Preaching in the Spirit

Preaching in the Spirit

DENNIS F. KINLAW

Francis Asbury Press
Distributed by Warner Press
Anderson, Indiana

W Warner Press, Inc.
PO Box 2499
Anderson, IN 46018-2499
800-741-7721
www.warnerpress.org

Cover design by Carolyn Frost.
Edited by Joseph D. Allison.

ISBN-13: 978-1-59317-522-1

Printed in the United States of America.

CONTENTS

PREFACE

I remember the surprise that came to me as I leafed through the religion section of a Sunday paper and found a headline that ran across five columns in inch-high black letters: "Greatest Story Ever Told—Told Poorly." And I thought, *Somebody has heard me preach and is writing about it.*

Perhaps you have felt that way about some of your pulpit efforts. I suspect that no people in the world feel as dissatisfied with their efforts as preachers do. Preachers habitually feel self-conscious when they have finished preaching, because who among us can ever do justice to the gospel? Yet it is part of the miraculous work of God that he uses the likes of you and me, not to mention the likes of our sermons, to accomplish his work. Through the foolishness of our preaching God chooses to save those who believe.

The things that happen in a preacher's personal life have a great deal to do with what happens when he preaches. He cannot preach effectively out of anyone else's experience; he comes out of his own. Some would tell us to ignore our own experience in the preparation of our sermons; but I believe our experience must be considered every time we step into the pulpit. Let me share some things from my own life that have affected the way I preach:

When I was thirteen years old I came to know Christ in a vital, victorious way. I had been a member of my parents' church for two or three years, having grown up in a devoutly religious family. My family took me to church every Sunday morning and evening, and occasionally (to insult me?) they took me to Wednesday night prayer meeting. But those were the days of an emerging Protestant liberalism, and I grew up with no consciousness of anything more than religious form and ceremony. Religion was just a part of life for me. Then one day I found myself in a place where I could not escape the presentation of the claims of Christ on me, personally. I was genuinely converted.

That conversion changed my life in two significant ways: First, Christ stepped out of history and out of religious institutionalism and became a living Person to me. Coming from my background in those religiously liberal days, I never expected to meet an intelligent, educated person who believed in the physical resurrection of Christ. But I suddenly had no trouble believing in the resurrection because I knew the risen Christ. I knew what life was like when he was there and what it was like when he was not there. That was a radical difference in my life.

Second, I had a new appreciation of Scripture. Of course, we read the Scriptures in Sunday school and church. My father, who had been converted, kept a Bible on his law desk. It was his pattern and my mother's to read the Scriptures every day. Before my conversion, I assumed that if I was to be a sincere Christian I should read the Scriptures, too. So I tried to read a chapter every day to satisfy my conscience. I might just as well have been reading the Greek multiplication table as far as edification was concerned; but I did it out of duty. The interesting thing is that, when God touched my heart, he touched my mind and I could understand Scripture as I never had before.[1]

The person who led me to Christ had given me a small copy of the Gospel of John published by Moody Press, a paperback book with a red cover and underlined in the right places. I put it in my shirt pocket and when I played ball my perspiration caused the ink to run; my mother began to complain about the red marks on my shirt. But I did not want to be without that little book because Christ had suddenly come alive for me through it. I did not think I could live without it.

---

[1] Authentic evidence that the Spirit of God has touched a person is to be found in the way he or she thinks as much as in the way he or she feels.

Nothing in the world is as significant to a preacher as the day Scripture comes alive for him—the day when Scripture seizes him, when he knows that it belongs to him and he belongs to it.[2] That happened to me early, and it made a radical difference in my life as well as my preaching.

Preaching never came easily for me. I was very shy and extremely self-conscious. There were times in the beginning when I would wonder as I sat on the platform if I would get to the pulpit. Worse than this was the fact that I was always very nervous. I suppose one of the reasons I learned to preach without notes was because I shook so much. But when the Word came alive in my soul, I wanted to share it. And when I had let God prepare me, I found release when I reached the pulpit. The anointing came and I was free.

That has brought me to the conviction that there is no more fulfilling experience in all the world than the sense that God's Spirit has taken you and dared to use you for God's glory. I do not think it is presumptuous to speak about this. Anyone who has ever experienced this anointing knows that it did not come from him or her; it comes from beyond. It is a given. It is all of God's grace.

Other things early in my life began to shape me. I will never forget an experience that I had when I, as a Methodist, found myself preaching in a Swedish Baptist church. It was not too long after my graduation from seminary. I preached that night on John 5:24, delivering what I thought was a pretty good sermon. It was an evangelistic series and when I gave an invitation, seven persons responded. That was surprising and satisfying to me.

But after the service, an elderly gentleman waited to talk with me. Tall, stately, and gray-haired with a gray mustache, his name was Otto Reidberg; that name is eternally written in my memory. He looked like King Olaf stalking down the aisle as he came to greet me. I reached out to shake hands with him, expecting him to say,

---

[2]Although both women and men serve as pastors and preachers, I usually have followed the traditional convention of referring to a pastor or preacher in the male gender, for the sake of simplicity.

"Thank you, that was a good sermon." But instead of shaking my hand, he firmly took me by the shoulders and gently rocked me back and forth. Staring me straight in the face, he said, "Son, Dennis Kinlaw doesn't know enough to help a soul. He's not that bright!"

I am sure my mouth dropped open in amazement, but he continued, "Son, this world doesn't need to hear what you think. What it needs to hear is what God thinks. Go home and get down on your knees with your Bible and stay there until you know what God thinks. And the next time you stand up to preach, tell people what God thinks."

I don't remember the end of that conversation. All I remember is that I walked out of that church with Otto Reidberg's words ricocheting in my mind. The next morning, I rolled out of my bed onto my knees, flipped my Bible open, and began to read Scripture with a new intensity and seriousness.

As I look back, I do not remember feeling at any point in that conversation that my new friend was being unkind or ungracious. There was such an authenticity in his manner that, despite the directness of it, there was an obvious tender concern in what he said. I am grateful for every day of seminary training that I ever had; but that one conversation with Otto Reidberg has been more valuable than any year of seminary training that I received, as far as empirical impact has been concerned.

Some years after that experience, I found myself sitting in a class in New Testament theology at Princeton Theological Seminary. (I had been preaching for a number of years and was now 31 years of age.) The course was taught by Otto Piper, a great scholar and a profoundly committed Christian. On Thursdays he would devote most of the session to answering questions. In one of those sessions, a fellow student said, "Dr. Piper, in a few days many of us are going to be finishing our work here and heading out into the pastorate. Do you have a list of 'must' books that every preacher should read?"

Old Dr. Piper's facial expression was normally a bit Sphinx-like. His face did not show a lot of expression when he spoke, nor was his tone very animated. He paused a moment before answering. Then he spoke in a simple manner that belied the significance of what he was saying: "I know only one 'must' book."

That was all he had to say on that subject. Now I certainly do not believe, nor did Otto Piper, that a preacher should read only the Scriptures; Oswald Chambers said the man who reads only the Bible never really reads the Bible. But the preacher is a man or a woman of one Book primarily, and everything else we read ought to be used to help us with understanding it. We need to study other things, but the Bible is the supreme thing. It is God's Word that folks need.

Dr. Piper turned to us one day and said, "You know, young men and young ladies, many people feel that Calvin and Luther produced the Reformation. But it wasn't Calvin and Luther. What happened was that when Luther read the Book of Galatians, he listened; and when he listened, it exploded inside him; and when the truth of Galatians exploded inside him, he didn't have any better sense than to go tell it to other people! A similar thing happened with Calvin. Calvin's congregation knew what he was going to preach on a given Sunday because he simply started with the verses following the one where he quit the previous Sunday."

The great tragedy of the Reformation, Piper said, was that when Luther died, Melanchthon edited his work. And when Calvin died, Beza edited his work. Melanchthon encouraged the people of Germany to read the Bible to find Luther's doctrine in it, while Beza encouraged the people of Geneva to read the Bible to find Calvin's. Thus the Word of God was stifled again.

That was a comment for which I will never cease to be grateful. I am a Wesleyan in theology, but I need to be very careful that when I read the Bible my concern is not to find what Wesley taught, but to discover the Word of God. If Wesley opens windows on the Word of God (and he does for me), three cheers for Wesley; but the important thing is that the Word of God comes alive for me, so that I can share it with others. It is the living Word that produces the kingdom of God. You and I are not going to build the kingdom; the living Word will do it. When that written Word is quickened by the Holy Spirit and becomes alive within us, we become instruments of the Spirit to do the Lord's work of evangelism.

I remember another day when Piper said, "I am afraid of you fellows and ladies who underline your Bibles." (I carefully closed mine at that point.) He said, "You don't have a right to choose which portions are the Word of God. What you don't underline is the Word of God just as much as what you do underline. You need to hear the whole Word of God, not the parts that fit your particular theology. In fact, I can tell you which verses most of you have underlined...." (He went right ahead and rattled off several passages that I had underlined in my Bible.) "Now I want to say to you," he stressed, "that you will never know the Word of God unless you know it wholly."

Two things about that comment fascinated me: One was the concept of the wholeness of Scripture. I was having trouble making sense of one paragraph at a time, and Piper was talking about taking themes—*motifs*—and following them throughout the totality of Scripture. I began to sense that I had a lot more work to do than I'd anticipated. Memorizing selected passages did not mean that I knew the Word of God; in fact, memorizing a text might well mean that I would lose it! Familiarity can breed blindness.

The second thing that impressed me about Piper's comment was the realization that he was talking about the Old Testament and the New Testament as equally important parts of God's revelation. My background caused me to look upon the Old Testament as inferior and less significant than the New. Slowly he began to indoctrinate me to the fact that nobody had a New Testament as we do until two hundred years after Christ, after the Christian church was well established. And if God could build a church in the first century without a New Testament, it would be negligent for us in the twentieth century to preach only out of the New. When Piper got through with me I registered in a beginning Hebrew class. And I will always be grateful! (I'm convinced that one of the reasons we Christians have not really transformed our culture is the fact that too often we have neglected the Old Testament. It ought to be a part of every preacher's knowledge reservoir.)

Another professor at Princeton was of great help to me; he was a Frenchman with a heavy accent named Emile Cailliet. (At times it seemed as if the best professors at Princeton grew up overseas and were graduates of the Princeton School of Broken English!) Cailliet, a philosopher, had been an atheist for years. He had married a Scottish Presbyterian girl but they had agreed that they would not have a Bible in their home. When their first child was born, all of the spiritual aspirations in Cailliet's wife came to her afresh. She began to think of what she wanted for her child. One day as she was pushing the baby in a pram, she passed a little Huguenot church and noticed that the door was open. She went in and found a venerable-looking gentleman who was the pastor. She said, "Do you have a Bible in French?" He smiled and gave her a copy. With some feeling of guilt, she put it in the baby clothes and smuggled it back into their home.

Without the encouragement and inspiration that Scripture gives to a believer, Cailliet had to seek a substitute. So he went through the literature of the ages and copied out any inspirational passage that he could find. These he put into a notebook for his own solace and encouragement, thinking that when his spirits were low he could turn to that book for strength. The day he finished his notebook, he sat down under a tree to enjoy his work. To his deep disappointment, he found that it did not really speak to him; this creation of his own carried no strength of persuasion. Dejected, he returned home and put his book on the shelf. At that moment, his wife walked in with the Bible. Apologetically, she tried to explain why she had gotten it; but Cailliet grabbed the book from her hands, rushed to his study, and began reading. He had never seen a Bible. He opened it by chance at the Beatitudes and began to read.

The result was shock and surprise. His comment was: "It found me out. It discovered me to myself." It was as if the One who wrote the book knew all about him. The result was a transformation of life that led to a change in vocation.

Cailliet's comment that the Bible "discovered him to himself" has shed light for me on a pivotal passage in the Gospel of Mark. The scene is in the synagogue at Capernaum. The account in Mark 1 records how, after Jesus was baptized by John and was tempted by Satan in the wilderness, the Lord came to Capernaum to begin his ministry.

> ...And when the Sabbath came, Jesus went into the synagogue and began to teach. The people were amazed at his teaching, because he taught them as one who had authority, not as the teachers of the law (Mark 1:21-22).[3]

Let me share with you how I understand that brief paragraph. We know that Peter was in the synagogue that day, since he took Jesus home with him afterward. His brother Andrew was probably there since we know that he was already one of Jesus' disciples. As Jesus spoke and the crowd felt the impact of his power and his wisdom, I can see Peter nudge Andrew and exclaim: "Andrew, did you ever hear a preacher talk like that before?"

And Andrew said, "Never!"

Peter asked, "What's so different about him?"

Andrew replied, "He makes sense. When did you ever hear a preacher who made sense?"

"You're right," Peter could have replied. "He sounds as if he knows who I am. He sounds as if he knows where I am, where I ought to be, and how I could get there! Let's ask him to go home with us."

That is the kind of self-discovery Cailliet was speaking about. It will discover us to ourselves, if we will listen. What the Bible tells us about the Jews or about the apostles or about the church is secondary; but what God shows us of *ourselves* through its pages is the real shock.

---

[3]Jesus teaches in the first chapter of Mark and preaches in the second chapter. There may be some significance in that sequence; perhaps a preacher's hearers need to be taught before they are ready to be summoned to a decision.

That must happen to us before we can preach effectively! All too often we preach about history and abstract values when we should be able to say, "The Word of God has come alive for me. Here's what it says about me and to me!" That's the point of being biblical in our preaching: We must present the Bible not only as the Word of God, but as the Word of God *about us*. Biblical preaching involves more than reciting and explaining the text. Most evangelical preachers can quote significant portions of Scripture, but that is not enough; Scripture must be presented in such a way that it speaks to the needs of the person who hears it. That can occur only through the enlightening power of the Holy Spirit. When the Spirit's internal revelation breaks into the preacher's mind and attends his preaching, it has the potential for radically transforming people's lives.

That's the kind of thing that Piper said took place in the Reformation. He said further, "There is enough undiscovered truth in the Scriptures to produce a Reformation and an evangelical awakening in every generation." Wouldn't that be thrilling? If we could find a way to let the Word of God come through us to influence our culture with that kind of power, we would find the fulfillment in our work of which we dream.

That's the vision of preaching that began to break across my own consciousness during my years at Princeton, the thing that I found myself praying could happen in our own country: the Word of God come alive and preachers like you and me becoming effective instruments of God's revelatory grace. Now for that to be true, something extraordinary must happen to the preacher, mustn't it? Something supernatural must happen in me and to me. That conviction with its challenge and its inspiration has lingered with me since those student days and has moved me in the preparation of the lectures contained in this book.

When I received the invitation to deliver these lectures at the Billy Graham Center, I remembered the comment of a friend who said, "Kinlaw, when fellows like you and me cast shadows of any length in this world, it's an indication of how late in the day it is." I felt humbled by the invitation, convinced that I had little original thinking to share with my co-laborers in the work of preaching. But I was delighted to accept the invitation because nothing has intrigued me more than the ministry of preaching. I am surely no expert on preaching; but it is exciting and satisfying to discover that, in what any of us render to God in sincerity, he finds something acceptable to use to his glory.

Dennis F. Kinlaw

1

Attachment By Detachment

The greatest problem in preaching is not the preparation of the sermon but the preparation of the preacher. We have an abundance of books and a raft of seminary courses on how to prepare and deliver the sermon; but scarcely anyone tells us how to get ourselves ready to do the preaching that God calls us to do.

Perhaps this is one reason why Scripture usually gives us biographical data about the great preachers. The biblical narrative introduces a Moses, for example, by telling something about his background: where he came from, what his experiences were, and his relationship with God. The same is true of Samuel, who merited very early in Israel's history the title of *prophet;* of Isaiah, whose life experience we know in significant detail; and of the apostle Paul who, every time he got into a difficult spot, began to tell the story of his conversion on the Damascus Road, thus leaving us with priceless personal information about himself. While we preachers are students of the Book, let us remember that we must be students of the person, too. I think that is why Scripture embodies the truth—even the truth about preaching—in personal histories of people who were remarkably like you and me.

As I read the biblical biographies of mighty preachers, I'm convinced that ultimately there is no great preaching unless the preacher partakes of the divine holiness in some measure. While worldliness may make a preacher clever, it will never make him powerful. The Bible illustrates repeatedly that in preaching, as in anything else a servant of God endeavors to do, "the Spirit gives life; the flesh counts for nothing" (John 6:63). The Spirit of the Lord within us can reach someone else with the gospel far more effectively than we can reach that person in our own persuasive eloquence. Our ministry must come out of our walk with God. We find a superb example of this as we study the call of the Twelve in the Book of Mark:

> Jesus went up into the hills and called to him those he wanted, and they came to him. He appointed twelve—designating them apostles—that they might be with him and that he might send them out to preach and to have authority to drive out demons (Mark 3:13-15).

Carefully note the reasons why he called these twelve men into the ministry. The order in which Mark gives his reasons is very significant:

He called them *first* of all "that they might be with him."

He called them *second* "that he might send them out to preach."

And he called them *third* to do works of mercy, epitomized by the act of delivering those who were oppressed by the demonic.

You will notice he did not call them first of all to be preachers; he called them first of all to be "with him." All of their other ministries were to originate out of that fellowship, that communion with Jesus. During the first three years of Jesus' ministry, they simply traveled with him. He sent them out to do evangelistic work on occasion, but that was not the primary purpose of those days. The chief purpose was that they might get to know him. And interestingly enough, in getting to know him they got to know themselves. At the end of those three years, he took them north to Caesarea Philippi and there they talked about who he was. Peter said, "You are the Christ [i.e., the Anointed One of God]" (Mark 8:29). Immediately after this confession, the apostles entered a new phase of intimacy with Jesus. As Christ had taught the multitudes before, he now turned his attention to his friends (Mark 8-10). He opened his heart to them on the long journey to Jerusalem. They now knew the mystery of his person, so he began to introduce them to the mystery of his mission, his passion. Now in deep intimacy with him they began to learn how alien their thinking was to his. The preaching of the years ahead would have deep roots in these quiet hours with him. Their ability to be redemptively involved with the world would grow out of this special intimacy with him.

The literal meaning of the word *apostles* is, "those who are sent." That concept of sentness implies two vital relationships: a relationship to the people to whom the apostles went and a relationship to the One who sent them. The Gospel of John explains that the apostles' relationship with Jesus was like that Jesus had with his Father. Notice what Jesus says to the Jews who criticized him for healing on the Sabbath:

> I tell you the truth, the Son can do nothing by himself; he can do only what he sees his Father doing, because whatever the Father does the Son also does. For the Father loves the Son and shows him all he does.... By myself I can do nothing...
> (John 5:19-20, 30a).

Here is the eternal Son of God, the second person of the Trinity, saying, "By myself I can do nothing." I used to think this was the human Jesus speaking; I don't believe that anymore in light of the statement, "...he can do only what he sees his Father doing." Jesus is talking about his relationship as the second person of the Trinity to the first person of the Trinity. If the eternal Son cannot do the work of God except in intimate relationship to and dependence upon the Father, it is certain that our only significant fruit will come as we walk with and lean upon the Spirit of the same God.

The doctrine of the Trinity allures me more daily; that doctrine states among other things that Jesus is the eternally begotten Son.

Now the verb *to beget* (to bear) is one that we normally use in a punctiliar sense. A birth date can be marked on the calendar; we can record on a birth announcement the very minute that the child is born. But the creeds speak about the One who is the eternally begotten Son, because what took place in Jesus' relationship to the Father is an eternal relationship. He is eternally being begotten.[1] He eternally draws his life from the Father.

Then Jesus says, "As the Father has sent me, I am sending you (John 20:21). If you want something to shake you up, live with that verse a little while! What Christ is to us, we are supposed to be to the world. That puts preaching in a rather important category, doesn't it? It's an awesome thing. Might this be the reason Jesus says, "...Whoever accepts anyone I send accepts me; and whoever accepts me accepts the one who sent me" (John 13:20)?

Might this be the context for Paul when he said, "For to me, to live is Christ" (Phil. 1:21)? In other words, Paul might have been saying two things with that statement: First, "for me to live is Christ because he's the source of my life." Second, "for me to live is Christ because I represent Christ to other people." To paraphrase that thought: "For me to live is for you to know Christ."

Some of us may back away from that understanding of ministry, but I think it is faithful to Scripture. This is why Paul speaks of our being "ministers of reconciliation" in 2 Corinthians 5. Look at that passage for a moment:

> For Christ's love compels us, because we are convinced that one died for all, and therefore all died. And he died for all, that those who live should no longer live for themselves but for him who died for them and was raised again.
>
> So from now on we regard no one from a worldly point of view. Though we once regarded Christ in this way, we do so no longer. Therefore, if anyone is in Christ, he is a new cre-

---

[1]This may be why even an atheist gets misty-eyed when he sees his child born; he is seeing a temporal manifestation of something that eternally takes place in the nature of the Deity.

ation; the old has gone, the new has come! All this is from God, who reconciled us to himself through Christ and gave us the ministry of reconciliation: that God was reconciling the world to himself in Christ, not counting men's sins against them. And he has committed to us the message of reconciliation (2 Cor. 5:14-19).

Paul sees the gracious love of God proceeding from the Father to Christ, from Christ to us, and from us to the world. The Reconciled and the Reconciler send us to reconcile. Christ's love compels us so that we now no longer can live for ourselves; we can live only for the One who gave himself for us. He died for us. Now we die to our way and, in living for the One who gave himself for us, we live for others for whom he gave himself. Christ has called us to be intercessors and mediators, to stand between God and the world. We have a mediatorial role as distinct as the one Jesus had. But it is not our work; it is his. He invites us to become channels through which he can work.

Of course, we do our mediatorial work with limited human equipment. But don't forget that for God to do his mediatorial work he too became a human. Don't disparage the effectiveness of a human ministry that originates in the Spirit. It is an incredible thing to be a human, an especially marvelous thing to be a human in the hands of God.

Your First Priority: Spending Time With Christ

Jesus spent more than three years with his disciples to get them ready for the task of ministry. The eternal God, engaged in the urgent business of saving the world, spent these years with twelve men, even though he knew he would lose at least one of them.[2] They

---

[2]It's interesting to note that Jesus chose Judas for the ministry, though Jesus was fully aware of Judas' readiness to betray him. Jesus said, "Have I not chosen you, the Twelve? Yet one of you is a devil!" (John 6:70). When Christ chooses us for his work, we cannot assume that we are spiritually strong.

were far more important to him than the multitude. As Christ's minister, you will always be more important to him than the multitude because there is no hope for the multitude apart from you.

Jesus says, "All that belongs to the Father is mine. That is why I said the Spirit will take from what is mine and make it known to you" (John 16:15). He draws his life, his ministry, and everything he has from the Father—and gives it to us.

Our perpetual temptation in the ministry is to let the ministry take priority over our personal walk with Christ. We are always conscious of the pressures to put the work first. That is so easy to justify. The reality, though, is that we always move from serving in his resources, gained from intimacy with him, to ministry that arises from our own strength alone.

Our security against such a drift is the development of personal devotional habits that keep him central and that maintain a perpetual influx of his life and power. We must know the resurrected Christ and commune with him each day.

When I think of this, I am reminded again of Emile Cailliet. He was a layman but occasionally led the morning chapel service. The format was basically a hymn, a Scripture, a prayer, and a hymn. There was not too much opportunity for the leader to display his creativity apart from the prayer; the chapel services were usually quite routine. It was different when Dr. Cailliet had the chapel. The students often flooded the room on those days because they wanted to hear him pray. No doubt his Einstein hairdo, his horn-rimmed glasses, and his thick accent contributed to their interest. The main thing, though, was reflected in his opening address to the Deity: "Our living Lord...." When we heard those opening words, the place was instantly electric with a sense of the divine presence. The miracle of worship was occurring.

If one has ever known that presence, he is also aware that he can lose it. Cailliet once recalled an experience he commonly had when lecturing in pastors' conferences. By the time of his third lecture he usually found himself besieged with pastors who wanted counseling. Their most common concern was the fact that the presence they once had known was now lost. The joy, the excitement, the drama of the ministry was gone because they had lost the sense of Christ's presence amid the pressure of their work.

Little wonder we have so many books for ministers about how to live with pressure and how to avoid burnout. This work can strip one apart. The pastor's common mistake is to turn to his work to relieve the pressure, rather than to seek Christ's presence for restoration and needed grace. Our work should grow out of our time spent with him, not the other way around. The freshness, the wonder, and the joy of his presence will make the pressures bearable.

The main reason we should learn to walk intimately with the Lord should never be utilitarian, though. The truth is that Christ wants to teach us the pure joy of that fellowship with him. He wants us to know that he is more to be desired than all of his gifts.

I was in my late thirties when I began to have some trouble with my voice. I was gripped by the fear that I might actually lose it. Preaching was virtually the only way I knew to support my family; that was all I had done since the day I graduated from college. What would I do if I could not preach?

Then the Lord began to deal with me about my fears. Did I not believe that he would care for me and my family? Early in our lives my wife and I had decided to take Christ at his word when he said he would care for those who put him and his kingdom first. We had claimed as our own Matthew 6:33:

> But seek first his kingdom and his righteousness, and all these things [food, clothing, and shelter] will be given to you as well.

So I asked God to forgive my doubts. Then I had a more disturbing thought: *But I don't want to quit preaching. That is the greatest thrill I have ever known. Preaching the gospel has been the most exciting and fulfilling thing I have ever done. I probably could not be happy if I were not able to preach....*

The inner voice of God's Spirit broke my reverie unexpectedly: "So my service means more to you than my presence! Am I not your joy and your fulfillment?"

Immediately I was stricken with guilt and found myself asking for God's forgiveness. I found myself saying, "Lord, if I never preach again, my peace will not be broken. You are my joy and my fulfillment; not your service." That was a liberating moment.

My voice problems cleared up and have never returned. I found a new freedom and a new joy, though, in knowing that his presence is even better than his service. He alone should be necessary for my fulfillment. He should be enough.

Abraham:
Model Of Our Faith Relationship

Have you ever noticed that Abraham is the prime biblical model of faith? When Paul wishes to illustrate the meaning of justification by faith, he doesn't use one of the twelve apostles or even himself; he points to Abraham. The same thing is found in the Epistle to the Hebrews, the Epistle of James, and various other Bible books. Why is Abraham the model? William James gives us a clue in his *Varieties of Religious Experience* when he indicates that we seldom see anything clearly unless we see it in exaggerated form; the daily ambiguities of life must be stripped away if we are to see starkly the essential things. Perhaps this is why the Bible constantly refers us to Abraham. Abraham lived long before Jewish institutional religion, before the law was given at Sinai. He demonstrated a faith that was not law-related, church-related, or lifestyle-related. What does God really want from a man? Not primarily obedience to the law, nor liturgical ceremony, nor a peculiar lifestyle. Abraham never preached a sermon nor wrote a page of Scripture, but he did walk and talk with God; and in that we see the essence of what God wants in his relationship with us—a friendship of personal intimacy and trust.

A friend of mine at the university had difficulty with that idea. He was a typical university kid—very bright and somewhat agnostic. He used to laugh and say, "Kinlaw, the Book of Genesis is so anthropomorphic. Just feature God 'walking in the cool of the day' with a man or a woman! Now if you can find one page in the Old Testament that reads like Aristotle, I'll be interested. I can grasp the meaning of a God who is an Uncaused Cause or a Prime Mover. Those concepts are not so crude."

I scoured my Old Testament to find him a page like one from Aristotle's *Metaphysics*. Then I thought, *For heavens sake, wouldn't I hate to live with an Uncaused Cause or a Prime Mover? I'm much more interested in Somebody who cares about me enough that he'd like to come and walk with me.*

I'm not boasting when I say that God wants to walk with me, because he wants to walk with you too. What an appealing idea!

I've come to love those opening three verses of Genesis 12, where God tells Abram to leave his native country and his own family for "the land I will show you." So Abram went out not knowing where he was going, but knowing *with whom* he was going. For a long time I wanted God to show me his will so I could decide whether I liked it or not. Yet each time God said, "I'm not interested in what you think about my will as much as I am in what you think of me. I don't want you to walk with my will; I want you to walk with me." I have found his will is always good; but the best thing about it is that I find him there.

I was already in the ministry when Elsie and I married. We have been in the ministry ever since. But I'm glad she didn't marry the ministry; she married me. In effect, this is what God said to Abraham: "I take delight in your attaching yourself to me, not to my will."

Almost every young person you counsel as a pastor wants to know God's will for his life. How much more important it is for him to know God than to know what his will is! If we know God, his will becomes evident. We can't miss it; it will come.

Abraham's life makes this point especially clear. God told him to leave his country, his household, and his family. Not because any of these things is inherently wrong; actually, they are normal "goods."

In these things we find our identity, our security, and our fulfillment. Yet God called Abraham to leave these.

Was God establishing a paradigm for us? I think so. He was saying to Abraham, "I want you to find your identity, your security, and your fulfillment not first in these relationships but in your relationship with me." He called Abraham from a life of attachment to the good into a life of attachment to God. I believe this made Abraham's life the human source from which the redemption of the world could come. In that life God gave the pattern for us all. We should not overlook the fact that out of Abraham's attachment to the Lord came a new land, a new family, and a new household—each of which was superior to that left behind.

Some Reflections
On The Preacher's Detachment

The pastor especially needs to be detached from the good. He needs an attachment to the Lord that is so strong that he is not possessed by his congregation. He needs to love his people and care for them. However, he needs that detachment which leaves him free to lead them rather than be emotionally dependent upon their support and their approval. If the attachment to Christ is not greater than that to one's flock, then the relationship between shepherd and flock will become destructive rather than creative. Only in the context of this detachment from his congregation will the pastor be free to preach the whole counsel of God.

If the preacher is to be faithful to the spiritual needs of his people, he must be willing to offend them at times. No sincere pastor wants to be offensive. Yet no pastor is truly free if he is not free to offend. The preaching of the gospel will sometimes hurt those who hear. It will expose their sin and their unbelief. It will lay bare their hidden idolatries. This process is never comfortable. It is the only way, though, to deliverance. That pastor loves his people best who loves Christ enough that he can speak faithfully to their need.

Our attachment to Christ should be the single *necessary* relationship in our pastoral lives. All other attachments should be secondary and contingent. Only then are we free from being corrupted by, or from corrupting (on our own initiative), those with whom we relate in secondary fashion. When God is really the God of our lives, all of our relationships are cleansed. When any other attachment threatens that primary commitment to him, all of our relationships are blighted.

Recently I received a phone call from a young woman who was seeking help for her brother. He had been divorced and was experiencing marital difficulties with his new wife, who had also been divorced. My friend said, "He came to see us again last night. He and his wife had just concluded a counseling session during which she said again and again, 'I'm through. I want to go away. I'm tired. I do not want to be bothered anymore.' The counselor said to him, 'Did you hear what she said?' His response was, 'Yes, but I don't want to hear it. I don't want to live alone.'"

My caller said, "We read Scripture with him and tried to help him. He was offended, though, and felt we were judgmental. How can we help him to get reconciled to his wife?"

I found myself answering, "Perhaps you should not. I wonder if any man is ready to be reconciled to his wife until he can live without her."

"What do you mean?" my caller asked.

"Until he can find enough grace to live alone, is he really worthy to be her husband? If he can't live without her, it is not a voluntary relationship. It is a necessary relationship. And a necessary human relationship is never ethical, is it?"

Only one relationship in life should be necessary, in the sense that we cannot live without it; that is our relationship with Christ. When we let anyone or anything other than Christ become necessary to us, the resulting relationship is inevitably sick and corrupting.

The literature of spiritual formation has much to say about this creaturely detachment. Too often, though, we tend to forget that the freedom we seek is spiritual and not geographical or material. We think that if we physically separate ourselves from our attachments we will be free. The Desert Fathers of the early church tried this. They felt that physical, spatial distance would release them from their human bonds. So they fled into the wilderness, only to find that distance did not cut their heart-bonds to the things they had left behind. Their appetites and attachments went along with them, for they learned these things are a matter of the heart.

François Fénelon understood this. He was a member of the court of Louis XIV, the tutor of the king's grandson, and a court preacher. He became the spiritual guide of many in that brilliant but gaudy court. He counseled them to seek a simplicity of life. But how could one live a simple life in that opulent social context?

Fénelon explained that simplicity is not as much a matter of externals as it is of the inner heart. A person may live in the midst of what the world sees as finery, yet be living simply within the inner heart because none of the externals are essential to his peace. The outer appearances of such a person are not contrived to feed his ego or pander to the taste of his peers. Such a detachment from things and opinions will lead to the freedom that every servant of God should have. Only then can one devote all of his psychic and spiritual energies to the glory of God and to the service of God's people.

The Hazards
Of Superficial Attachments

A true attachment to Christ should transform all other attachments. It should save us from superficial relationships that strip us of time and energy, and in the end are unfruitful. We need divine perceptiveness here to keep us from exploiting (or being exploited by) one another.

George MacDonald contrasts a healthy relationship with an exploitative relationship in his novel, *The Tutor's First Love*, in which he describes two young ladies from whom we can learn a great deal. One is a peasant girl and the other a jaded worldling. Both are in love with the same man, the rich girl's tutor, while the tutor is enamored with the worldling. All three live in the same house. The peasant girl has that depth of soul and attachment to God that allows her to suffer her love in silence and wish her beloved true happiness. She has something more important in life than getting what she wants. The sophisticated girl is manipulative and cunning. In the end, though, her own selfishness destroys the tutor's love. Then she begins to see the true nobility of the peasant girl, who has the resources to try to help her erstwhile rival put her life back together.

As the weary young sophisticate opens her heart and shares her personal history with the servant girl, both become aware that it is no history at all. It is merely a meaningless recital of superficial attachments in which the young lady's motivation was always to get and never to give. She permitted people to draw close enough for her to use them and strip them of what she wanted, but never close enough to receive from her as freely as they gave. She had loved and possessed—and lost. The peasant girl was free to give because she did not have to possess.

The pastor can learn from such a story. It is easy for the relationship between the preacher and his people to be corrupted by possessiveness and exploitation. In early Methodism no preacher ever received a salary; he was to receive "pastoral support." The Methodists keenly saw a theological difference between the two. The preacher was not their hireling. He was not to be dependent upon his people. They were to be responsible for him and attend to his physical needs, as he was responsible for ministering to their spiritual needs. The relationship was one of free responsibility, not necessity.

It is very easy for a congregation to come to feel that they "own" their pastor, that he works for them; yet it is impossible to minister to people who feel that they own you. Ownership means having the right to control. In that respect, only God should own the preacher; it should be God alone for whom the preacher works. Only then can the preacher be free enough to serve his people with integrity.

The missionary Amy Carmichael said, "The vows of God are upon me," and her ministry came out of that divine call. We should serve God by ministering to our people, rather than serving our people by telling them about God. Some may feel these are only verbal distinctions; but they are real differences.

This is why a sense of divine calling and divine presence is so important. It keeps us conscious of the One whom we serve. The vows of God are upon us! An awareness of that will keep us going when otherwise we would falter.

My Methodist friend John R. Church once said, "The first sermon I ever preached had 36 points in it, and when I stood up I couldn't remember a single one of them. I had to sit down in total humiliation; my mind was a complete blank. It was a little country church in the mountains of North Carolina, and as soon as the service ended I went running out the door. My father finally caught up with me. He came down the dirt road with his lantern and walked beside me in solemn silence for several minutes. Finally, he said, 'Son, God knows you can't preach. I know you can't preach. Now the whole community knows you can't preach. For God's sake, don't put the family through that again.' "

John Church said, "I looked back at him and sobbed, 'Dad, I'm sure that you know I can't preach. I know I can't preach. The church knows I can't preach. But if God knows I can't preach, why doesn't he take the burden off me? Dad, *I've got to preach!*' "

And preach he did. He became one of the most effective evangelists in this country. John's ministry was marked by power and fruitfulness. Why? Because he was not preaching for the church or for its people. He was serving God. And there is a distinct difference.

When we are detached from everything else and attached to the Lord, our calling becomes clear. His work then is a thing to be savored. The nature of the One who calls and sustains us will give dignity and nobility to our work. Such a relationship is prerequisite to effective preaching. In fact, it is prerequisite to Spirit-anointed ministry of any kind.

Father, I want to know Thee, but my coward heart fears to give up its toys. I cannot part with them without inward bleeding, and I do not try to hide from Thee the terror of the parting. I come trembling, but I do come. Please root from my heart all those things which I have cherished so long and which have become a very part of my living self, so that Thou mayest enter and dwell there without a rival. Then shalt Thou make the place of Thy feet glorious. Then shall my heart have no need of the sun to shine in it, for Thyself wilt be the light of it, and there shall be no night there. In Jesus' Name, Amen.

—A. W. Tozer[3]

---

[3]A. W. Tozer, *The Pursuit of God* (Harrisburg, Pa.: Christian Publications, 1948), p. 31.

2

Called To Work With God

David Livingstone had been fleeing all day from hostile, infuriated savages. During his sixteen years in Africa he had never been in such peril. Now facing what appeared to mean certain death, he was tempted to steal away under cover of night and seek safety for himself. But he sat down at a riverbank and turned to the Scriptures for guidance. Note the entry in his journal:

January 14, 1856. *Evening.* Felt such turmoil of spirit in prospect of having all my plans for the welfare of this great region and this teeming population knocked on the head by savages to-morrow. But I read that Jesus said: "All power is given unto Me in heaven and in earth. Go ye therefore, and teach all nations and *lo, I am with you alway, even unto the end of the world.*" It is the word of a gentleman of the most strict and sacred honor, so there's an end of it! I will not cross furtively to-night as I intended. Should such a man as I flee? Nay, verily, I shall take observations for latitude and longitude to-night, though they may be the last. I feel quite calm now, thank God!

Note the words underlined in his entry. They were evidently underlined in his heart. He was not alone; he was accompanied by the sovereign Christ to whom all power, not only in heaven but at that spot in Africa, was given. Such a man as Livingstone should not flee because of the One who was with him.

Our calling as preachers is not to work for God but *with* him. We are not called just to be his servants; we are called to be his friends. There is a radical difference between the two. In John 14-16 we get Jesus' most intimate expression of his relationship to his disciples. Note that in the fifteenth chapter he describes them as his friends:

> My command is this: Love each other as I have loved you. Greater love has no one than this, that he lay down his life for his friends (John 15:12-13).

Jesus knows that the next day he will go to the cross and lay down his life indeed. For whom will Jesus lay down his life? He says, "For my *friends*." And he goes on to define what he means when he says his disciples are his friends:

> You are my friends if you do what I command. I no longer call you servants, because a servant does not know his master's business. Instead, I have called you friends, for everything I have learned from my Father I have made known to you (vv. 14-15).

What an astounding statement! The thing that impresses me most about it is the quality of the relationship between Jesus and his disciples, including you and me. Jesus is not interested in keeping secrets from us. He says, "What my Father has given me I give to you." He expects us to be in a relationship with him such as he has with the heavenly Father. We cannot be one with him ontologically, for he is Deity and we are his creatures. But we may enter as far into becoming one with him as our creaturehood will permit, and he wishes to become one with us as far as his nature will permit.

Dante's *Divine Comedy* presents a magnificent allegory of the Christian disciple's growing relationship with his Lord. An event that occurs near the end of that narrative gives a striking insight into man's relationship with God.

Dante has nearly completed his pilgrimage. The journey that

began so lugubriously in hell is now behind him; the mountain called purgatory has been climbed. When he began its ascent, his weight was so heavy he could scarcely raise his lower foot to the level of the one above. But with the mountain of purgatory behind, he swiftly moves up through the empyrean toward God. Beatrice journeys with him; she has led him all this way.[1] As they move up through the heavens he looks away from the beloved one who has brought him so far.

His instant guilt at looking away from Beatrice is countered by her response. Charles Williams says, "This—disturbs her?—to laughter." Her joyous laughter at being forgotten arises from her own sense of fulfillment. She has achieved the highest goal a creature can achieve: She has been the means of pointing another creature to the Creator of all, to God.

Dante moves on up toward the presence of God. There he sees three concentric circles, each with a different hue, but all occupying the same space. The second circle (the Son) mirrors the first (the Father). The third is a flame (the Holy Spirit), breathed equally by the first two. He takes a second look and sees in the second circle the image of himself. Notice how Williams describes Dante's vision:

> At the depth of hell Satan chews men; but at the end of Paradise the great mathematical symbol shows Man distinct yet in-Godded.[2]

What a fascinating counterpoint to the Creation narrative! When God finished his creative work, he saw in man the likeness of himself. Now at the end of the process of redemption, man looks at the

---

[1]Note that in this instance a woman is leading a man to an encounter with God. Also note that Dante had fallen in love with Beatrice while they were yet children, and the whole story had emerged from that relationship of masculine/feminine attraction. Beatrice expressed her fondness for Dante by bringing him to the throne of God; her human love brought him to the point of experiencing divine love.

[2]Charles Williams, *The Figure of Beatrice: A Study in Dante* (New York: Octagon Books, 1978), p. 223.

second person of the Godhead and sees the likeness of himself. Creation made man like God. Redemption made God like man.

Dante's vision has many philosophical and theological implications. We know for example that God is the eternally unchanging One; yet God has eternally changed his condition by incarnating himself in human flesh. How else could the One without flesh and members commune with the physical beings he created? And now he wills that we share the glory of the Godhead with him (cf. Rev. 1:13; 14:14). This is an awesome reality that cannot be fully comprehended by God's creatures, not even by the angels.

The Principle Of Coherence

The intimacy of the relationship that God seeks with man is indicated in many ways by Scripture. In the Gospels, Christ speaks of our being one with him and his Father. It is not the metaphysical oneness of philosophical mysticism, but the oneness of self-giving love.

This has special significance for the preacher. As mentioned earlier, we are to have a relationship with Christ as Christ has with the Father. His relationship with the Father is revealed in passages such as these:

> Believe me when I say that I am in the Father and the Father is in me;... (John 14:11a).

> All that belongs to the Father is mine... (John 16:15a).

> I am not alone, for my Father is with me (John 16:32c).

> I and the Father are one (John 10:30).

> ...Understand that the Father is in me, and I in the Father (John 10:38b).

> ...Anyone who has seen me has seen the Father (John 14:9b).

> He who receives me receives the one who sent me (Matt. 10:40b; cf. Mark 9:37).

To receive Christ is to receive the Father, and to receive the Father is to receive Christ. Language like that used to describe the relationship of Christ to the Father is also used by Christ to describe our relationship to him. Note:

> My prayer is…that all of them may be one, Father, just as you are in me and I am in you. May they also be in us so that the world may believe that you have sent me…. That they may be one as we are one: I in them and you in me (John 17:20-23).

> I tell you the truth, whoever accepts anyone I send accepts me; and whoever accepts me accepts the one who sent me (John 13:20).

The relationship of the believer to Christ is such that what one does with one, he may be doing with the other. This is what Charles Williams would call the law of exchange or coinherence.

John Donne rightly said, "No man is an island…." Modern individualism is built on an illusion, an unrealistic understanding of what personal existence really is. No one lives to himself. To be a person is to receive. No one originates his own life or sustains it by his own power. Our fulfillment is never in ourselves. Each of us is part of a web of reality, an intricate complex of coinherence.

The pattern behind human relations is ultimately that found within the blessed Trinity. So we should regard with eager interest what Jesus says when he speaks of our relationship to him being like his to the Father. Our patterns of relationship are to be found in God, not in a broken human society.

This has relevance to the work of the pastor as the representative of Christ. He stands in God's stead. He acts out the immanence of God by his daily involvement in the sufferings of his people. The pastor has the privilege of entering redemptively into their lives. Shared suffering is at the heart of pastoral ministry, as the pastor takes the burdens of his people into his own life and thus helps to alleviate them. He can never liberate his people from their burdens if he is unavailable or impervious to them.

I know I am broaching a subject that is touchy with a lot of pastors. I've heard many of my brethren in the ministry say, "I don't have time to be involved with visitation, counseling, and hospital work. My place is in the study." Some of my pastoral colleagues become very sensitive when I start asking about their involvement with their people. So be it. I think it is time to challenge the rationale that says, "My role is to be the pastor-teacher, the resident intellectual for this parish." That rationale permits a pastor to stand in a superior position and speak down to his people or, worse, to speak across the chasm.

Some interpret Ephesians 4:11 to mean that pastors are called solely to train the saints to do the work of ministry. Yes, I think the pastor is called to train his people; and yes, I think all the members of the body of Christ are ministers. But I reject the rationale of a pastor who says, "I am the trainer but not a participant. I am the coach who stands on the sidelines and cheers the team on, but I never get in the line of scrimmage; I never get involved with the knocks and bruises and broken bones of everyday Christian life ."

I wonder how Jeremiah would have felt about that pattern. I believe Jeremiah is a primary model of pastoral ministry. After Jesus had spent three years healing the sick, cleansing the lepers, giving sight to the blind, and doing all other sorts of miraculous things, he turned to Peter and said, "Who do they think that I am?" And Peter replied, "Some of them think you're Jeremiah...." That is surprising, to say the least. Six hundred years before Christ, Jeremiah stood against the tides of decay and apostasy that were to pull his nation apart; yet he never performed a miracle or knew an hour of success. But later, when Christ appeared, the Jews were reminded of Jeremiah. What was the perceived similarity? I think it was their *personal identification* with the sufferings of their people. If a pastor's ministry involves no personal identification with the lives of his parishioners, it really isn't Christian ministry in the full sense of that term. If a pastor is not willing to expose himself to the hurts of his people, he has not taken Christ as his pattern.

In the Gospels, the teaching of Jesus is never separated from his involvement with His fellowman. He always speaks to human need and ministers out of the context of human need. His example challenges the modern notion of the pastor-teacher. Jesus gave us the model of a pastor-shepherd. Obviously, no man can do all the shepherding work in a local parish. But if he keeps himself aloof from the everyday struggles of his people, they are going to keep themselves aloof from him.

A Further Repudiation Of Modern Individualism

Paul states in 2 Corinthians 6 that we are called to be "workers together" with Christ. This passage includes one of the *sun-* words coined by the New Testament writers which does not occur in classical Greek; the Greek prefix *sun-* denotes the idea of being "together with" someone else. Here are some examples:

Fellow prisoner [lit., "prisoner with"] (Col. 4:10)
συναιχμάλωτος
Reclining at the table with (Luke 14:10)
συνανάκειμαι
Bearing with (Rom. 8:26)
συναντιλαμβάναι
Fit together (Eph. 4:16)
συναρμολογέω
Reigning together (2 Tim. 2:12)
συνβασιλεύω
Fellow traveller (2 Cor. 8:19)
συνέκδημος
Chosen together with (1 Peter 5:13)
συνεκλεκτός
Quickened/made alive together with (Eph. 2:5)
συζωοποιέω
Bear evil treatment along with (2 Tim. 2:3)
συγκακοπαθέω
Endure adversity with (Heb. 11:25)
συγκακουχέομαι
Agree/consent with (2 Cor. 6:16)
συγκατάθεσις

Co-inheritor/fellow heir with (Rom. 8:17); also translated
as *Have the same body with* (Eph. 3:6)
συγκληρονόμος
Fellow imitator of Christ (Phil. 3:17)
συμμιμητής
Stand in line with/correspond to (Gal. 4:25)
συστοιχέω
Be of one mind with (Phil. 2:2)
σύμψυχος

I would love to see a scholarly article on the theological mentality that produced these words in the New Testament. The New Testament writers thought so differently from their pagan world that they had to coin their own vocabulary, a wide array of *sun*-words, to express their unique view of man's relationship to God. They repeatedly emphasized that we are in this experience of life with God, that God is in it with us, and that we are in it with each other. It is a view that stands in striking contrast to modern individualism.

The writers of the Old Testament used similar phraseology to reflect the relationship of Yahweh and Israel. God promised to be with them; he would be their God and they would be his people. The seal was to be his presence with Israel, in their very midst. His presence made Israel, Israel. Note the word of Moses:

> ...What else will distinguish me and your people from all the other people on the face of the earth? (Exod. 33:16b).

The center of their life was the tabernacle (later the temple); and the heart of the tabernacle was the Holy of Holies where Yahweh was supposed to reside. God was there to protect, to guide, and to sustain his people. But more importantly, he was there because he loved them and wanted their fellowship.

The level of intimacy that Yahweh sought with his people is seen in the fact that he talked face-to-face with Moses "as a man speaks with his friend" (Exod. 33:11). And what Yahweh achieved with Moses he seems to desire with all people.

The God Who Stands And Waits

One story illustrating this intimacy is often overlooked. It is found in Genesis 18, which describes how Abraham entertained three strangers, one of whom was God himself. Twenty-four years had passed since God had promised Abraham a son. Now God tells Abraham that the coming year will see the birth of that child of promise, Isaac. This is significant news, for that child will be the means through which the Savior of the world will come. The saving God visits Abraham this day. His concern: the salvation of the world. His means: through the family of Abraham and Sarah.

As they finish their conversation, they walk to the edge of the camp. Yahweh decides to discuss with Abraham his problems with Sodom and Gomorrah. (One is reminded of the words of Christ in John 15:15: "...For everything that I learned from my Father I have made known to you.'") The text says:

... But Abraham. remained standing before the Lord (v. 22).

Then begins Abraham's intercession for Sodom (the city in which his nephew Lot and his family live) and Gomorrah. This text clearly implies that Abraham initiates that intercession.

However, a footnote to this verse in the NIV suggests this may not be what the Hebrew text originally said. Scribal tradition indicates that the original text said:

And Yahweh remained standing before Abraham.

We know that the Hebrew text was considered sacred by the Jewish scribes. No scribe copying a manuscript would dare to change the text. He could not even correct an obvious mistake by a previous scribe. He could make a notation in the margin, though. This was called $k^e t \hat{i} \underline{b}$ ("written"). The text itself was called the $q^e r\acute{e}$ ("read"). Often the marginal notes (the $k^e t \hat{i} \underline{b}$) were essential to reading the text.

At about eighteen points in the Old Testament, however, Jewish tradition tells us that the scribes did change the text. These are called the "emendations of the scribes" (*tiqqûnê hassôp'rîm*). One of these is reflected in the NIV's footnote for Genesis 18:22. In other words, the original reading of the text meant that Abraham did not initiate the intercession for Sodom and Gomorrah, but Yahweh did. The scribes assumed this reading was incorrect, so they emended the text at this point.

What if the scribes were wrong, however? What if the original reading was correct? The closing verse of the chapter (v. 33) is supportive of this understanding. It reads:

> When the LORD had finished speaking with Abraham, he left, and Abraham returned home.

The internal evidence as well as the scribal tradition indicate that this reading is correct, that it was not Abraham who initiated the intercession but Yahweh.

Why would the scribes feel obligated to change the original text of verse 22? Because they did not think it befitting the sovereign God, the king of all the earth, to stand before one of his subjects. Kings sit on thrones; their subjects bow before them to make supplication. Men plead with sovereigns, not sovereigns with men. The scribes felt the original reading would convey the wrong impression about Yahweh, so they "corrected" the text.

But does the original reading convey the wrong impression about God? The saving God who came for a cross, who took a basin and towel to wash human feet, is not above taking the supplicant's place to intercede for two great—though wicked—cities. We often underestimate how far God will go to redeem men and women. And we always underestimate our importance to him in that saving process.

This study of the emendations of the scribes has changed my understanding of that scene in Genesis 18. No longer do I see Abraham standing before God, initiating prayer for two great cities that the Lord plans to destroy.

Rather I see the saving God, who has just put into place the last piece of his plan to begin the messianic line through which the world is to be saved, standing before his friend Abraham. God wants to save rather than destroy. And so he waits plaintively before his creature; it is he who pleads with Abraham.[3]

This study has also changed my understanding of intercessory prayer. How many other times has the Lord stood before his church pleading for his world, and we never even knew he was there!

Some mornings I wake up and think to myself, *Kinlaw, you don't pray enough. There is a lost world outside. You ought to care more. You ought to pray more.* My conscience quickly concurs, so I make time for prayer that day. I feel better. I congratulate myself for thinking such noble thoughts and praying.

Now I am convinced that the truth is quite different. The sovereign God stands in the shadows of my conscience, saying, "Kinlaw, there really is a lost world out there. Don't you care enough to stand with me in prayer so that perhaps it can escape judgment?" But when I hear his voice, I am so numb that I think it is my own.

Amy Carmichael tells how she wearied of fighting for the temple girls of India. The opposition to her work was so strong and the forces that bound those girls were so evil that she wondered if she could carry that sense of responsibility any longer.

> At last a day came when the burden grew too heavy for me; and then it was as though the tamarind trees about the house were not tamarind, but olive, and under one of these trees our Lord Jesus knelt alone. And I knew that this was His burden, not mine. It was He who was asking me to share it with Him, not I who was asking Him to share it with me. After that there was only one thing to do; who that saw Him kneeling there could turn away and forget? Who could have done anything but go into the garden and kneel down beside Him under the olive trees?[4]

---

[3]What was God's long-range purpose? Not judgment; he is the eternal Savior! He must destroy Sodom and Gomorrah in the process of redeeming the world; but that does not obscure his ultimate purpose.

[4]Amy Carmichael, *The Gold Cord* (New York: Macmillan, 1932), p. 31.

God wants to save the world, and he looks for helpers. The realization of this fact has changed my attitude toward prayer and toward preaching. I now realize that the preaching event is not my service, but his. He wants to accomplish certain things in that service; I am simply privileged to be his accomplice. I am privileged to work with Him rather than for him.

The Barrenness Of Working For God

Working *for* God means that we try to think what he wants done and then go and do it for him; when we finish, we expect to have his approval and reward. The unconscious emphasis of such thinking is upon the preacher himself, upon how well he is doing his work, upon how competent he appears to be.

This may explain why many pastors' conferences focus on techniques more than on the relationship between the minister and the Lord. There is an implied assumption that if you know the "nuts and bolts" of sermon preparation and church administration, you will be a successful pastor. This is tied to the idea of working for God—carrying out an assignment—rather than being his co-laborer in ministry.

Leaders of such conferences remind me of the professors of the old psychology-of-religion school, who could explain conversion but never could produce it. If the Lord isn't in our ministry, our efforts amount to nothing. "The flesh profits nothing," Scripture says. What we do is "flesh," even when we do it correctly and it appears to the world to be successful. It profits nothing unless the Lord is in it. Certain preachers have a reputation for being "successful," and other pastors hanker to be like them, even though they are spiritually barren in God's sight. We need to walk closely enough with Christ that we can see as he sees.

In this respect, we should see spiritual significance in the Bible's many stories that revolve around barren women. Sarah, Rebecca, Hannah, Manoah, Elizabeth—all were barren until "God opened the womb." The prophet Isaiah uses this figure to address spiritual barrenness. He says that when the Lord returns to his disobedient people, they will be like a barren woman who is suddenly able to conceive:

'Sing, O barren woman,
    you who never bore a child;
burst into song, shout for joy,
    you who were never in labor;
because more are the children of the desolate woman than of
    her who has a husband,' says the LORD
                (Isa. 54: 1).

I find a similar message in Isaiah's allusions to dry places that become fruitful (e.g., Isa. 35:1-2; 43:19-20; 51:3). The dry places of the wilderness have everything necessary for producing a fruitful crop, except the moisture. The moisture alone won't produce fruit, of course; but neither can soil without the moisture. God reminds us again and again in these passages that if we are to have any spiritual fruit, any spiritual offspring, it will be because of what he is doing—not what we do.

When the minister becomes the pivot around which his ministry revolves, the results are deadly. The Lord will not be fully present in any ministry where the minister gets the glory. The Holy Spirit comes to exalt Christ, not to exalt you and me. Anything that draws attention to our cleverness, our brightness, or our competence is ultimately sterilizing. This is why we must ever remember that we are called to work with him.

A Sanctified Conscience
And Spiritual Sensitivity

In the press of daily ministry, it is easy to lose that perspective. But the Holy Spirit can enable the preacher to see as Christ sees. This is why each of us needs the baptism of the Holy Spirit, the same baptism that came to the disciples at Pentecost.

The Spirit will quicken a preacher's understanding and enable him to see the difference between working for God and working with him. The unsanctified Christian will tend to take pride in working for God, saying, "See what I did for him." He thinks God ought to be in his debt. But with the Holy Spirit's baptism the minister receives a sense of total and continual dependence upon God that precludes such vain ideas. The Spirit makes a minister realize that God alone gives the increase; there is a sense of *sola gratia* in ministry as real as in salvation, so that the preacher wants Christ to be preeminent.

John R. Church was a young and aspiring preacher when he was invited to give the commencement address at Asbury College in the 1930s. He took the invitation seriously and prepared diligently. He later told me, "The place was packed. Excitement was high. God was with me and I soared. I thought, *I have this audience in the palm of my hand. I can do anything I want with them.* Suddenly, a cold chill moved over me. I closed the service immediately, went to my room, and got on my knees. I said, God, if you'll forgive me, I'll never be guilty of that again.

"For years afterward, I met people who said, 'Dr. Church, do you remember when you were at Asbury for commencement?' It happened so many times that I knew what was coming. They would say, 'You know, I have never heard such oratory.'

"I would ask, 'What did I preach about?'

"I never met a person who could recall the text or topic I had preached about," Dr. Church said. "All they remembered was the oratory."

See the integrity of a man who knew when he had crossed a line he was not supposed to cross? Some people think the sanctified life is one in which a person never errs; but when we seek God's grace to live a holy life, we know that's not so. As much as anything else, the sanctified life is one sensitized to error. Most of us would have walked away from that commencement service saying, "I did well, didn't I? God, you should be pleased with me today." But Dr. Church went away repentant. No one else in the crowd knew what had happened, but he knew. He went to his room and asked God's forgiveness for what the audience thought was magnificent.

The mark of a clean heart is *what you do* when you've slipped across the line of spiritual integrity. A lot of preachers don't even know when they have done that. Such is the difference between preaching about the Spirit and preaching in the Spirit. If we are going to work with Christ, we must be sensitive to his Spirit.

A certain friend of mine who is a very effective preacher has suffered some psychological problems. (I suppose that if I had his personal background, I would be suffering psychological problems, too.) He used to call me periodically on a Sunday morning and say with a trembling voice, "Dr. Kinlaw, there's no way I can preach today. I'm not worthy...." Then he would give me a catalog of all the sins he had ever committed. He would say, "I can't preach. Is there any hope for me?"

That happened over a period of years. My wife became weary of his phone calls because they occurred at some of the most inopportune times, but I tried to counsel him as best I could. Eventually, I found myself falling back upon this line of reasoning: "George,[5] what were you going to preach about this morning?"

"About Christ," he would reply.

"Do your people need to hear about Christ?"

"Yes."

"Do you know anything about Christ that they need to hear?"

"Yes."

"Then I believe you had better go ahead and tell them," I would conclude. "He will be there if you speak about him and he will do his work."

You and I cannot build the kingdom of God; only Christ can. Yet the only way Christ can accomplish that work is through preachers like us. Christ certainly can use a preacher much more effectively if he is a clean instrument; but in any case, if a preacher knows the truth about Christ, he ought to proclaim that truth to his people. Why? Because they need to hear the truth and because the call of

---

[5]Not his real name.

Christ rests upon him. As Peter Böhler once said to John Wesley, "Preach faith until you have faith."

The call to preach comes not because we are worthy, but because Christ has a world to save and he has no one else to help him in the task but you and me. When we stand in the pulpit, we must be aware of the fact that we are there by virtue of his saving power and his call to the ministry, not by any virtue of our own.

Every preacher fights the sort of doubts that my friend George faced each Sunday morning. You have fought them if you are a preacher. Yet there is great comfort in knowing that Christ is effectively at work in the preaching event, whether you feel you are effective or not. You have the opportunity to work with him. As a preacher, you have the privilege of getting close enough to him to find out where he is and what he is doing, and then meshing into his work. That is when preaching is fruitful. That is when lives are transformed through preaching.

3

Built Together
For God's Dwelling

In one of the first congregations I served I had a lady who was an excellent critic of my work. She would knock at our parsonage door at a quarter to seven in the morning to "see if the preacher was starting his day right." She always brought a basket of fresh peaches, melons, or some other kind of produce; so I couldn't get too upset with her! But that old lady watched over me. She corrected my grammar each week and pointed out things in my demeanor that were not as graceful as they should be. Though irritating at times, she was a gift from God.

One Sunday she was talking with me about another preacher. She said, "'His preaching is like dried peas on a tin roof." I thought, *Dear God, is that what she thinks of me?* But ever since I have been haunted by that image of dried peas being poured on a tin roof—noise without significance—and I have been reminded that, if the proclamation of God's Word doesn't come out of an intimate walk with him, it will be empty words instead of the living Word.

My daughter recently heard a certain evangelist whom I've followed with interest for several years, so I asked, "Honey, how was his sermon?"

She said, "Dad, that fellow must have spent some time in his prayer closet." Now my daughter hasn't attended seminary; she's the energetic mother of four kids. But she knows the difference between Spirit-anointed preaching and "dried-pea" preaching. Most of the people in your congregation will know the difference, too.

In order to prepare ourselves for a Spirit-sanctioned experience of corporate worship, we must catch the New Testament vision of the church. You are familiar with that passage in Ephesians where the apostle Paul speaks about building the church. He says,

> ...You are no longer foreigners and aliens, but fellow citizens with God's people and members of God's household, built on the foundation of the apostles and prophets, with Christ Jesus himself as the chief cornerstone. In him the whole building is joined together and rises to become a holy temple in the Lord. And in him you too are being built together to become a dwelling in which God lives by his Spirit (Eph. 2:19-22).

Underline that closing statement: "And in him you too are being built together to become a dwelling in which God lives by his Spirit." This can give fruitful insight into the dynamics of a worship service; everything we do in a worship service can be understood best in light of this verse.

The verb translated as "built together" *(συνοικοδομέω)* is a passive voice verb form. The word does not occur in classical Greek and occurs only here in the New Testament. Its passive voice stresses that fact that God builds his church and we are the materials that he uses. Now I think this is especially clear when we consider the act of worship; if the Lord's presence is not there, our preaching is merely "dried peas on a tin roof." If his presence is not with us, all of our efforts will lead to pure sterility and fruitlessness.

I have come to a fresh appreciation of that passage in Matthew 18 where Jesus says, "For where two or three come together in my name, there am I with them" (v. 20).[1] It is the Lord that our parishioners need, not you and I; but only as we come together in his name is the Lord going to appear to any of us. And so I find myself anticipating the preaching service with real eagerness. The Lord has never broken his promise: When we come together to talk about him, he comes into our midst. He comes! And he comes to do some wonderful things for us. His promise applies to every aspect of a worship service, including the delivery of the sermon. When one Christian proclaims the Word of God to another, the Lord meets with them.

Sensing God's Presence In Our Corporate Worship

I have always been awed by the way an unbeliever may be sensitive to the Lord's presence in a way that believers are not. I remember a young man who came into our services from a very pagan background. His father was an alcoholic, and by the time he was nine years of age this young man's mother made him go to help her drag his drunken father out of the bars and carry him home. He was taught early to steal to help support the family. (I do not think that he knew it was wrong to steal until after he was born again; there was no guilt connected with it in his mind.) Soon after he and his wife started attending our church, he came to me and said, "I need to talk with you."

I had to make a trip so I said, "Why don't you go with me, Dave?"

I will never forget riding along the New York State Throughway, west toward Utica, with this young fellow looking over at me. At last

---

[1]Jesus makes his controversial statement about "binding and loosing" immediately preceding this verse: "I tell you the truth, whatever you bind on earth will be bound in heaven, and whatever you loose on earth will be loosed in heaven" (v. 18). How can a disciple of Jesus loose anyone from sin? That can occur only when the power of God flows through him. And how can God loose anyone from sin? He has no way of influencing the sinner's life except through you and me. We will consider this intriguing statement in more detail in the Epilogue.

he said, "You know, there's something about this church that I don't understand, something I've never experienced before. I got trapped into coming. My wife made me come. But when I got in there something happened to me that I can't explain; I felt something I've never felt before. Is that God?"

Isn't that fascinating? Some so-called Christian people sitting right next to him didn't know that God was there. But he did. Dave didn't know who God was; but he sensed God's presence in the midst of worship.

I was preaching for a friend who is the senior elder at a church in one of our major cities, a church that has about three thousand people in attendance each Sunday morning. As my friend described the appointment on the phone, he said, "I want you to realize this is not an ordinary service. This really is not a worship service.'"

I said, "Wait a minute. You mean to say the 9:00 and 11:00 services on Sunday morning are not for worship?"

"That's right," he said, "at least not in the traditional sense. It's no place for Bible exposition and exegesis, for example; you'd have to tell these people who Matthew, Mark, Luke, and John are. In fact, some of them may still have the glaze in their eyes from their Saturday night activities." He said, "Kinlaw, this is not even evangelism. This is pre-evangelism evangelism."

I said, "Okay, if Sunday morning is not the worship service, when do you worship?"

"Well, we worship on Wednesday night. That's when the Body meets."

I said, "How many people do you have on Wednesday night?"

"Last week we had 1,000."

"How many people do you have on Sunday morning."

"Last week we had 3,200." After a moment of silence, he said, "Kinlaw, four weeks ago, we baptized 250 persons on one day."

This fellow's description of his church fascinated me. "Well," I said, "what sort of preaching do you think is appropriate for pre-evangelism evangelism?"

"For goodness' sake, don't give an invitation," he urged.

"Why not?"

"These people still think the believers are responsible for evangelism; they think that's the laypeople's job. So for goodness sake, don't corrupt them. And if you can preach half tongue-in-cheek, it will be that much better."

(If I had not known who was speaking to me, I would have been offended!)

I asked, "What other counsel do you have?"

"Try to find some point of identification with the people," he responded. "Make it personal, so that the people sitting out there will feel that you at least know who they are and what they are like."

So I went. At the end of the service, a very handsome young black man and his lovely wife came up to me. (I found out later he was in a high-tech business.) He said, "Sir, how long are you in the city?"

"I fly out this afternoon."

"Oh, too bad," he sighed. "I hoped that I could...that we could talk with you this afternoon. Could we talk with you now?"

"Well, let me shake hands with a few people here," I said, "and I'll get free as quickly as I can.'"

After the crowd dispersed, I found them sitting on the front row of the auditorium that had held over three thousand people that morning. I pulled up a chair and looked into their faces. The young businessman began hesitantly. "Patricia asked me what I wanted to ask you about, and I didn't know how to answer her because...well, because something happened this morning that's never happened to me before. I think it's what she's been doing her best to tell me about, and I've not been willing to listen to her. But it's happened to me now. And I don't want it to stop. What do I have to do to keep it going?"

Now that's not human work. That is not psychological manipulation. That's the Holy Spirit who comes when the body of Christ meets together and the Word is preached. He makes us conscious of Christ. Jesus promised us this would happen. If we walk with him and live with him and preach his Word, we ought to expect it.

The Dynamics Of A Spirit-Filled Worship Service

The most casual attenders will find something beautiful about a genuine worship service; but what is the source of that beauty? They say there's a special power in the service; but what is the power? It isn't power in the abstract, of course; it's Jesus' presence in the worship service. Even glib people know that something happens when he is there; but what happens? I think that question must be answered with some theological precision.

The doctrine of original sin states that when Adam sinned, all of mankind fell from communion with God and all have been dead in trespasses and sins ever since. Thus we are incapable of making an effort to move toward God. If we are ever to be saved from sin and its penalty, God must cause us to seek that salvation. We are utterly lost unless God causes us to seek him. That's why we can continue in our sin for years with little sense of guilt for what we are doing. But one day we become aware of God's presence and suddenly we "experience something we've never experienced before— conviction, remorse, and the desire to respond to God. If we respond affirmatively to him and confess, repent, and believe, we experience the thrill of knowing that we are forgiven and justified before God.

The pattern for our worship was established on Sunday evening after the Resurrection, the first time the disciples had come together after the crucifixion. Friday night had been one of desolation and despair; Saturday had been the most frustrating day of their lives; and now on Sunday they had begun to hear the amazing stories about Jesus' being alive again. You can imagine the leap in their hearts. So when the sun began to set on Sunday, what did they do? They looked for each other. And when they came together, what did they talk about? Jesus, of course. And while they were talking about him, he kept his promise. He had said, "If two or three of you gather together in my name…" and before they finished talking, there he was.[2] That's the pattern for us. That's the miracle of worship—the fact that he comes into the midst of hungry, seeking people and we sense he is there.

Guilty In The Presence Of God

One morning a lady called me for what seemed to be an idle chat. She had been attending a Bible class on Genesis that I was teaching, but she was so flippant over the telephone that I felt insulted. I started to hang up on her, but I thought, *Now wait a minute. Why is she that flippant?* So I said, "Jean, I'm coming over to see you," and in five minutes I was punching her doorbell.

As I walked in and sat down in her living room, I said, "Jean, what's wrong?"

"It's that lousy Genesis class," she growled.

"What's wrong with that Genesis class?"

She looked at me and exploded into tears. "It was eighteen years ago," she sobbed. "I thought it was all over. I thought I had forgotten it and perhaps everybody else had, too. But sitting in that Genesis class, it's as fresh as if it had happened yesterday." With that, she began to acknowledge her guilt and her need for forgiveness.

Many people commit sin without a tinge of remorse. Then God comes near and they feel guilty. If a preacher tries to produce the guilt, it's deadly. For how can one human being judge another? How can his condemnation help another to be healed? But if God produces the guilt, it has the potential for resurrection and regeneration.

If we preachers are honest, we will acknowledge that we too have been dead in our trespasses and sins. Who has not known days, maybe years, when he sinned without great concern? Who has

---

[2]This episode at Emmaus gives me a special fondness for Sunday evening worship services. In fact, I can make a better case for holding Sunday evening services that I can for Sunday morning, since that is the way it all began. Regardless of when we meet, though, Jesus comes if we meet in his name.

not known other days, perhaps years too, when he lived with great guilt but found no resources to break the powerful hold of evil on his life? Yet many of us also have known what it means to have the Spirit of Christ draw near. Then our powers that were paralyzed (Paul would say "dead") were quickened and we could choose what on other days we could only dream about. When he draws near, we find freedom to think, feel, and act in ways that in ourselves alone are impossible.

Our son Denny gave a very graphic account of that bondage to sin at a father-son banquet for our church, where he and I had been invited to speak. It was a rare moment for me; I never expected to hear my son speak in public because he was so shy and self-conscious. Yet Denny stood up, head down and speaking quietly:

> As most of you know, I grew up in a Christian home, a pretty good home. Very early, I heard about Christ. When I was seven my mother prayed with me to receive Christ. I have some very precious memories after that, of Jesus being very real to me. [I had never known that.] But when I began to approach that great chasm of inferiority that we call adolescence—when my Adam's apple was entirely too big and my muscles weren't nearly big enough—I began to be more conscious of me than of him. And he moved to the margin of my life.

> I got into college and decided that Christianity was simply one of the religions of the world, that really there wasn't a God. I never told anyone I was an atheist but I was quite proud that in my inner heart I had the courage to disbelieve God.

> Finally, I got into the university. I decided, *Ah, now I'm with people who are open and free.* I was shocked to find they were neither open nor free. I sat in a science class where a shy little girl suggested that the world may have originated through something more than simply the natural processes of evolution, and I watched the professor humiliate her. My professors were not open, nor were they free. They wanted to impose on me a view of reality that neither fitted what I had learned in my family nor what I had learned about life on my own.

I began again to open my life to God and he came back to the center. I decided that I wanted my life to be his wholly.

Then I began my hospital internship and residency. I found I could work 36 hours without a break, without sleep, just like the other guys could. But I had no time for God. I also discovered that when I didn't talk to God, he didn't talk to me. He moved to the margin of my life again.

When he moved to the margin, the hole that was left didn't stay empty. The place he had occupied now filled with appetites and passions. Slowly I discovered they were there and were controlling me. I began to feel sorry for myself. I looked at these other doctors with their private planes and their summer homes and their winter homes and their places at the beach and their big automobiles and their luxurious living, and I thought, *Just let me get out in suburbia and I'll make me some money and I'll have a chance to enjoy some of those things.* Slowly, it began to dawn on me that those appetites controlled me. I realized that, barring a miracle, I was already preprogrammed for disaster.

I had a day off. So I spent it alone, fasting and praying. [Elsie and I never knew about this.] I wouldn't recommend that to you if you're not ready for some changes in your life.

Six weeks later, the other surgeon's hand slipped and I was given plenty of time for God. Three of us were operating on a girl who was a drug addict. She was loaded with a form of hepatitis often found in drug addicts and prostitutes. When another surgeon's hand slipped, his instrument penetrated my glove and cut into the flesh of my hand. In due time I contracted hepatitis of the worst kind.

Those next few months were a time of great pain and despondency. I looked death straight in the face. But the funny thing is, I hardly remember the despondency and the pain and suffering. What I do remember is that the Lord came back to the center of my life. And when he came back, he set me free. The tyranny of those appetites was broken.

I asked him to heal me and he did, but not in the way I expected. I thought he would heal me in such a way that I would have a guarantee of tomorrow; I expected to bounce right back to my old routine. But that didn't happen. I asked him about that and he said, "I didn't give the apostle Paul a guarantee of tomorrow; why should I give you one?"

You know, that experience transformed my way of living. I don't take each day for granted anymore. I don't take my wife, my children, or my work for granted anymore. I take every one of them as a special gift from him, a gift of his grace. There are some mornings as I ride to work in Lexington that I watch the sun rise and find my cheeks wet with liquid gratitude for the new day. It's a free gift of his love, for me to enjoy and worship him. You know, it's not a bad way to live.

He sat down. Imagine how difficult it was for me to say anything meaningful when I had to follow that! But what interested me about Denny's testimony was the statement, "When the Lord moved out, appetites and passions moved in, and I was not in control." The sinner is not in control of himself; appetites and passions rule him. How will he ever get free?

The Sinner's Deliverance

Calvin and Augustine answered that question with the doctrine of predestination. Concerned that Christians should understand that salvation is not by human works but by divine grace alone, they said that it is by divine choice that men are saved, not by human choice. God in his grace chooses some to be saved. These he touches and quickens. That quickening causes them to seek him.

If you accept that view, then preach it fervently and expect God to touch somebody. But I think there is a better way to explain the biblical truth concerning salvation.

There can be no question, after reading the Bible, that salvation is all of God. On the other hand, the Scriptures seem to hold the man who lives in sin responsible for his lostness. But how can he be held responsible if he is unable to initiate his deliverance? I once thought the resolution to that tension lay in the fact that man has the power to accept Christ or reject him. I thought free will was a basic human ability that everyone possesses.

Slowly I began to question that view. If man could choose on his own initiative to accept Christ, then he would be initiating the process of salvation. Yet Scripture and experience taught me that man is much more bound in his sin than that view would suppose. Man may be free to make choices in morally indifferent areas—he is perfectly free to choose chocolate ice cream over vanilla, for example—but when it is a choice to challenge his own autonomy and rebellion against God, he is not free but bound. More deeply imbedded in man's sinful nature than the instinct for self-preservation is the inner demand that he keep control of his own life. Self-surrender is impossible apart from Gods grace. A man is not free to choose Christ apart from grace. So it is easy to see why Calvin and Luther came to their conclusions about "sovereign decrees."

But there is another way of understanding the dynamics of moral choice. True, man has no capacity within himself to challenge the tyranny of his sin. But there is a quickening grace of God that is to be distinguished from his saving grace. John Wesley called it "prevenient grace," the grace that comes before grace. Here is how it operates:

Through his Spirit, Christ draws near the sinner who is bound in his sin. Christ touches and quickens the sinner. The sinner's power of choice, so long bound by his sinful self-interest, is made alive once more. Now the sinner has a freedom to choose that he did not have until Christ drew near. That freedom itself is not salvation; but now the sinner is able to choose not to resist the Christ as he comes to save. Apart from that quickening touch, the sinner would not even know that the Savior had drawn near. Now by grace he can respond to the Savior who loves him and wants to save him. When God's prevenient grace moves upon a person's heart, he is released from the hold of the sin that binds and blinds him—released enough that he can make a free choice. And choose he must. Even the power *not* to say no to God is a gift of grace from God himself. This is what Charles Wesley meant when he wrote:

> Long my imprisoned spirit lay
> Fast bound in sin and nature's night.
>
> Thine eye diffused a quickening ray;
> I woke-the dungeon flamed with light!
>
> My chains fell off, my heart was free,
> I rose, went forth, and followed Thee.

When Christ draws near, blind eyes begin to see and the chains of sin loosen. Then and only then, in the near presence of Christ, does a person find the freedom to follow Christ.

So when that sinner comes into your congregation, lost in his trespasses and sin, the Savior draws near in love, warmth, and grace. The Author of life re-quickens the life of that sinner enough that he has the capacity to let the Savior come in. God's grace enables an unbeliever to respond affirmatively to the One who's taken the initiative to reach him. We should pray that that work of grace will occur while we preach. Otherwise on the ordinary Sunday morning it's impossible for someone in our audience to get saved. Jesus said, "No one can come to me unless the Father who sent me draws him" (John 6:44). Redemption is God's work. He's the Savior; we are glad to be his instruments, but we must remember that he's the Savior. We have the privilege of working *with* him. But it is he alone who saves.

The magnificent thing is that it takes place at all. The marvel of preaching is that the Lord deigns to come into our presence, not because we deserve an audience with him, but simply because he has promised to come. Wherever we worship him "in spirit and in truth," he's there. You and I are in the business of working with him to produce moments when belief is possible, moments when people can be redeemed and set free. What a responsibility we have! Yet what high privilege.

How To Prepare For
Spirit-Filled Worship

If people are to make commitments to God as they hear our preaching, we must be concerned about our preparation for worship. The Spirit of God must be free to work in the worship service. How can we prepare the way for him?

Prayer is the first way. I have never known a real work of grace in which someone had not prayed beforehand. John Wesley said that "no one is ever saved unless someone has prayed," and the preacher should be foremost among those who pray for the lost. How does this kind of prayer work? I don't understand all the mystery of it, but I have a story that may shed some light:

Early in this century, we had a most remarkable Methodist bishop in the southeastern United States named Arthur Moore. He was by far one of the greatest bishops of this century in the Methodist church. He was a railroader before he answered the call to the ministry, so he was accustomed to rising early. (We are told that his wife locked him in his study with a quart of milk at 6:00 every morning and wouldn't let him out until noon. Blessed is the minister who has a wife like that!) Moore became an effective witness and pastored some of the largest Methodist churches in the South before he became a bishop. Over a period of several years, he had the privilege of seeing somebody genuinely converted every Sunday that he preached—Sunday after Sunday after Sunday.

One of Moore's friends was visiting his church on a particular Sunday and they were discussing his great success as an evangelist. "How do you do it?" the friend asked.

Moore said, "Come with me." He took the visitor to the basement, where a prayer meeting was in progress. About seventy men were fervently praying for their pastor and for the worship service that was about to begin. When they finished, they quietly walked up the stairs into the service. Arthur Moore turned to his friend and said, "Notice where they sat."

His friend was puzzled. "What do you mean? They are scattered all over the congregation."

"Yes, thank God," Moore replied. "And where each one of them sits down, he's such a center of divine warmth that anyone frozen in sin who sits near him is liable to thaw out before the service is over."

Moore was using earthly language to talk about eternal and spiritual things, but I like his way of expressing it. Whenever you get a sinner into a congregation of believers who are spiritually warm enough and concerned enough, he's likely to "thaw out" for the Lord. That's why a pastor and his people should be intensely interested in prayer, entreating the presence of the Holy Spirit for each worship service.

Second, the preacher can prepare for Spirit-filled worship by making sure that he himself is filled with God's Spirit. God's work is done "'not by might nor by power, but by my Spirit,' says the Lord Almighty" (Zech. 4:6). The Hebrew words *chayil* ("might") and *koach* ("power") are used in the Old Testament to represent almost every kind of human resource, including physical strength, material wealth, and human talent. Yet how often we preachers say, "If we had the strength, if we had the wealth, if we had people with the gifts, if we had the other resources, we could get the job of evangelism done." All of those things are ruled out by Zechariah 4:6. Not by might, nor by power, nor by other human resources will God's work ever be done; only by God's Holy Spirit can the work be done.

We must be instruments of his Spirit. As A. B. Simpson said, "We are empty possibilities until He gets us." Every person we will meet is an empty possibility—an eternal possibility, but empty—until the Spirit touches and quickens and enters him. So if we wish to be about our heavenly Father's business when we step into the pulpit, we must be traffickers in the Holy Spirit more than traffickers in biblical knowledge or the skills of oratorical suasion. I do not disparage either of those things, nor other things that assist us in the work of wooing women and men to Christ. But I am convinced that we must put our relationship with God ahead of everything else, because he must be at work in the congregation as we speak. We must preach in the power of his Spirit if we are to preach with eternal results.

4

Relating
The Written Word
To The Living Word

We have seen that the person who preaches for commitment must be a man of the Word, that his ministry should come out of his walk with God, and that he should work with God rather than simply for God. The Spirit-filled preacher must have some sense of what God is doing in his congregation and how he meshes into that work. Now the fourth thing I want to say is this: The Spirit-filled preacher knows how to relate the Word of revelation to the Word in creation.[1]

No matter what a teacher says or how impressively he says it, if there is not some *extrinsic* witness to what he is saying, nobody will believe it. God made us questioners by nature,[2] because he is the God of truth and he does not want us to be deluded. This is why

---

[1] I am inclined to avoid using the phrase, "the Word in creation," for we could become sidetracked in a discussion about how much of God's truth is revealed in the creation of God. But even the theologians who are the most hostile to the concept of natural revelation end up with something comparable to Emil Brunner's "address-ability of the creation," the concept that God's creation is capable of receiving the Word which comes by revelation. So there is sufficient compatibility between the two schools of thought to allow me to use this phrase with comprehension.

[2] I used to think that the Devil had built a special doubting mechanism into my mind and that if somehow I could get it exorcised I could be a believing Christian. But

God gave us the tendency to question every statement that purports to be truth, especially when it comes from a single voice. But he confirms the revelation of his truth through several sources.

God has disclosed his truth to us through a natural revelation (the created world) and through a supernatural revelation (Scripture), and the two are in harmony. Scripture is confirmed and strengthened by our experience of the natural order. Conversely, Scripture interprets the truth revealed by the natural order; biblical principles explain why life goes wrong.

The *Chicago Tribune* recently published a series of articles on child abuse, incest, child prostitution, and related evils. The series ended with an editorial that raised the question of whether there really is more incest and child abuse than in earlier days, or whether it is simply more permissible to pull these matters out of the closet and talk about them now. The editorial concluded that it really doesn't matter.[3]

It is rather difficult to believe that we live in a culture where a prestigious paper like the *Chicago Tribune* can say that the question of whether there is more child abuse, incest, and prostitution in our society than formerly *does not matter*. Journalists treat these problems as if they were inexplicable anomalies. They have lost the ability to differentiate between right and wrong; thus they must treat moral questions as if they were irrelevant issues. Though such acts are not good in their eyes, they have lost the ability to call them *evil*. (Nonetheless, such things trouble the public enough that journalists will devote a series of articles or an editorial to discussing them.)

Life ceases to make sense when we turn away from God and the Scriptures. Then we can only compare ourselves with ourselves, and the qualitative differences between us are relative. Only when we

---

the same process that brought me to doubt also brought me to faith; so I learned that doubt is simply a negative faith. The capacity to doubt is put into us by God because God hates delusion.

[3]What medical society would not be interested in whether there is a growing incidence of a deadly disease?

include God in our thinking do we have a basis for making firm moral decisions. Only when we listen to God, as he speaks from Sinai and Calvary, can we really think in terms of right and wrong, good and evil. Yet even when we choose to ignore the revealed truth of God, something within us insists that there is a qualitative difference represented by the words *good* and *evil*.

Traveling on a plane one day while I was the president of Asbury College, I found myself sitting next to a young man who was a graduate student in sociology in one of our state universities. We were looking for a Christian sociologist at the time and I was having trouble locating one. So I thought, Maybe I can learn something from this fellow. I said, "Could I ask you some questions?"

He said, "Sure."

"Do you like sociology?"

"Love it."

I said, "Going to spend your life in it?"

"Yes."

"Well, I am a novice and an outsider. But it is my understanding that a sociologist cannot use the categories of good and evil, true and false, right and wrong, when he works as a sociologist. Is that right?"

The graduate student sat there for a moment, thinking. At last he said, "Yes, that's right."

"Now, let me get this straight," I said. "Why can't you use the categories of right and wrong, true and false, good and evil as a sociologist?"

"Well," he said, "We have to be objective. And how can I within my sociological system pass a moral judgment on what takes place in another sociological system? As a sociologist I cannot."

"In other words, as a sociologist you cannot act as if there is an objective moral order out there."

He thought for a moment and said, "Yes, that's right."

"Then let me ask you a question," I said. "If there is no objective moral order, why do we all feel guilty at some time or another?"

He said, "That's a tough one, isn't it?"

"Now you say you are going to spend your life in sociology. Why?"

He said, "Because there are so many blooming things wrong in the world!"

You know, it was forty seconds before he started turning red. And as he did, he looked at me and said, "You trapped me, didn't you?"

"No, I didn't trap you," I said. And I didn't. I had not thought about how the conversation was developing; it was totally unwitting on my part. (I'm not that clever…but the Holy Spirit is.)

I was fascinated by the fact that a budding sociologist felt obliged to act professionally as if there was no difference between right and wrong, good and evil. Yet when he had to make a decision as a human being, he could not operate without the very categories that his social science told him to ignore. My friend said to me, "There's so much wrong with the world." I didn't say it; I didn't have to draw the moral for him. The living, internal Word of the Holy Spirit brought him to that conclusion. Made in the image of God, he could not live without God's categories, though as a sociologist he felt obliged to ignore them.

The Consequences Of Ignoring God's Categories

When the radical distinction between the creation and the Creator is lost, the other distinctions most essential to the meaning and purpose of life go too. God's categories are crucial to the things that really matter. The unbeliever bears witness to this as much as the believer, if we have ears to hear and eyes to see that testimony.

William Barrett clearly demonstrates this in his provocative work on existential philosophy, *Irrational Man*. His chapter on aesthetics, "The Testimony of Modern Art," resembles the writings of Francis A. Schaeffer (though it was written several years before Schaeffer's work on aesthetics). Barrett points out the flattening of planes in modern art and the flattening of climaxes in modern literature.

He reminds us for example that Western painting has traditionally had a central subject to which the surrounding space is subordinate. Rembrandt's *Christ at Emmaus* is illustrative: Christ sits with Cleophas and his friend at table; while Jesus breaks the loaf of bread, subdued light plays on his hands, so recently nailed to the cross and now breaking bread for his own. The hands and bread are central, while the other details recede into the shadows.

Contrast that with a modern cubist painting. All pictorial climax is gone. All space in the picture has equal significance. Negative spaces in which there are no objects are just as important as the positive spaces with their contours of physical objects. If the figure of a person is treated by the painting, the body may be broken up and distributed over the canvas. There is no clear center. All is discrete. It is the art of the anticlimactic.

Thus a modern artist may paint a checkerboard in which red squares are as significant as black and black as red; he may as readily paint a madonna and child or a clothesline stretched across an alley between two tenement buildings in a slum. All are equally illustrative of life. All are of equal significance.

Or take the flattening of values represented by James Joyce's novel, *Ulysses*. There are 734 pages in which all of the movement is horizontal. The traditional concept of a plot is absent. The classical pattern of the novel, in which the story begins at a certain point, rises to a climax, and then declines to a resolution (the form represented in Aristotle's *Poetics* and so determinative for Western literature) is gone. One can begin reading Joyce's novel on page 1 or page 101 or page 201 or page 301 with no loss, so far as plot or story (in the traditional sense) are concerned. One finds merely a stream of consciousness, and the plane on which it moves is flat. The element of transcendence is gone.

Barrett acknowledges that modern art and literature reflect a view of reality quite different from what they have traditionally reflected. No longer is life seen as a coherent and logical system. Barrett believes this change expresses a basic change in modern man's world view. He has no interest in going back to the styles of the past; but he would like to find a means to "redeem any part of our world." He suggests that perhaps this may be achieved, as modern art has attempted, "by exalting some of the humble and dirty little corners of existence." Perhaps the most telling statement in Barrett's chapter is the quotation with which he begins it. The words come from W. B. Yeats:

> Now that my ladder's gone,
> I must lie down where all ladders start,
> In the foul rag-and-bone shop
> of my heart.

Modern man may reject the notion of a world above but he still finds himself talking about "ladders."

Letting The Unbeliever Draw His Own Conclusions

If you invite an unbeliever to think about his situation and talk about it, out of his own mouth you will hear a confirmation of biblical truth. Earlier in this century, E. Stanley Jones wrote a book entitled, *Is the Kingdom of God Realism?* The thrust of it was, "I am a Christian because my cells tell me that is the way I am made to live." Anyone who listens to the gospel long enough and candidly enough will understand what Jones meant. We are made by our Creator for the Kingdom of God.

In preaching we ought to remember that when we preach biblical truth something inside our listener will say, "That's right." Something within bears witness against him. There sat my sociologist friend saying, "You tricked me," when he knew that he bore witness against himself. When we stand before God in the Judgment, there will not be a single soul in the world with an excuse; and many there will say, "How under the sun did I miss it?" Life itself will bear witness against us. We have this advantage in preaching the gospel: The external witness of God's created world confirms what we say.

I was sitting one day at a wrought-iron table for a luncheon at a very lovely home in Florida, next to a swimming pool. There were four of us at the little table, including Sally, the daughter of the family we were visiting. Sally was a mother in her thirties. As the conversation progressed, I began to suspect that Sally was a Christian. I knew that her parents had not been Christians long, so I asked, "'Sally, how did you get into this family?" (I didn't mention which family I was talking about, but she knew instantly.)

She looked up and said, "It wasn't easy. You see, my father was an alcoholic, a Thursday-night-to-Sunday-noon alcoholic. But between Monday morning and Thursday afternoon, he made enough money that we lived very well.

"He was occasionally religious," she explained. "He'd go to church once in a while. I always figured he went because of his guilt. But with my mother it was another story. She was a pagan. She never had any guilt, so she never went to church, and as a result I never went to church.

"Here in the South everybody is a Southern Baptist, and Southern Baptists won't leave you alone," Sally chuckled. "My husband and I carefully instructed our children that if anybody asked them what their religion was, they were to reply 'We're Jews.' I knew that would keep those Southern Baptists off our backs. (After I became Christian, I had to teach our children they were *not* Jews.) I think back to some of the conversations my mother and I had before we became Christians, and they were so nearly blasphemous that I shudder to recall them.

"When I was twenty I fell in love with a wealthy young man. We had the perfect country club wedding. We seemed to have everything going for us. But we hadn't been married very long when I knew something was wrong. My hostility toward my husband deepened until I said to him one day, 'Dan, if you loved me, you would walk out and never come back. The happiest moment of every day is when you walk out that door in the morning, and the most miserable is when you come back at night. If you loved me, you'd leave and never show up again.'

"But he did love me and he wouldn't leave me. Finally I thought, *Maybe it isn't all his fault. Maybe it's the neighborhood.* [That's how blind and fallen sinners are.] So I raised that question with Dan and he said, if it would help, we would move. So he bought a lot in the newest, loveliest section in the city and built a dream house for me. I had everything I could ask for.

She said, "I hadn't been in that house two weeks until I knew nothing had changed. Worse, I found out there was a religious woman living five doors down the street. (I told my informative neighbor, 'Thank you for telling me. I'll steer clear of her.') You can imagine my horror when I found that the religious woman was in the same car pool with me and was going to be transporting my children to school. The inevitable day came when that religious woman pulled into my driveway with my kids in her car. She got out and walked over to me and said, 'How are you?' Don't ask me why, but I found myself saying, 'What do you mean?' And the religious woman looked back and said, 'How are you? How are you, really?' And I exploded into tears."

Sally said, "The next thing I knew, I was sitting in my living room and that religious woman was sitting in one of my chairs, saying, 'There's a hole in you so big that nothing in creation will ever fill it, but Jesus. '"

I was intrigued by what Sally told me next. She said, "When she told me that, something inside me said, 'There it is! You've been waiting all your life for this moment. *Now someone has finally said it.*' "

That's the Word at work in creation. Sally was made by God to serve Christ. She was made to receive the eternal Word. And when somebody presented him, she said, "This is it! My native habitat." She had been a foreigner, an orphan, an outsider; but her Christian neighbor brought her into the family of God.

Christ isn't a plus value that we add to life. He is life itself. You and I have the privilege of presenting to people the One they seek, though they may not know they are seeking him. We have the privilege of relating the written Word to the living Word, who is at work in the experience of every man and woman. Once they recognize him, something inside them says, "I was made for this."

They may not admit it; apart from the quickening touch of the Holy Spirit, they cannot know it. But the living Word fits—he fits their experience like nothing else can.

This theology of general revelation will be determinative of our preaching. If we don't understand this theology, our preaching will be superficial and manipulative; but if we do understand it, our preaching will be a third force that brings the witness from the world together with the witness of the Word.

The Preacher
An Interpreter Of Modern Man

By the same token, a preacher should seek to understand humanity as much as he possibly can. He ought to be an interpreter of his time, able to explain where mankind is at this point. That's what Augustine did. First, in his *Confessions*, he spelled out what he saw God doing in his own life. However, because he was a bishop, a shepherd of souls, he was responsible for explaining what God was attempting to do in the life of the church. As he saw the ravages of secularism upon the church, he tried to interpret the larger purposes of God in history. Augustine knew that Scripture was one witness to God, but human history was another. The result was Augustine's book, *The City of God*, perhaps the greatest theology of history ever written. This book contains Augustine's meditations on the fall of Rome.

Alaric and his Goths had sacked Rome in 410. This brought consternation to the civilized world. Rome was the symbol of stability and order for Christian and pagan alike. So in 413 Augustine wrote *The City of God* to interpret that event in terms of the larger purposes of God. The book brought a word of consolation, comfort, and hope. Its influence is still with us reminding us that the temporal city of man is not our ultimate dwelling. It is the city from above, the city of God, that will prevail.

In writing this book, Augustine is a model for every Christian. A Christian should lift modern man's eyes beyond the transitory, beyond time and history, to the eternal. Only then can people be freed from the enchantment and the allure of the world that ensnares them. A Christian should be able to show that human history bears witness to the ultimate purpose of God.

Read the sermon Augustine preached the Sunday after he heard that Rome had fallen. Malcolm Muggeridge's series of films on the history of Christian thought devotes an entire episode to that sermon.[4] Augustine discerned where mankind was in its pilgrimage toward God and he interpreted that pilgrimage in his sermons. His work has laid a shadow across the subsequent one thousand years. An astounding thing! All preachers should be interpreters of the contemporary state of man, which is an important aspect of the Word that is in creation.

Every preacher should be in some measure an interpreter of where man is before God. He needs to know the witness of anthropology and history. If he can relate those witnesses to the biblical word, then he can speak of where man is as well as who man is, to where man is becoming as well as what he ought to become. Scripture enables the student of man to take the data of the social sciences and find meaning that those sciences could not otherwise give. Nowhere is this more obvious than as we study the meaning of personhood; biblical revelation helps us interpret the data that the natural study of man affords.

Interpreting The Meaning Of Personhood

What is a person? The British philosopher John Macmurray, in the Gifford lectures of 1953-54, contended that the great crisis of twentieth-century thinking is in the realm of the personal. The loss of so much of the world to communism symbolizes the fact that we Westerners do not know what a person is; therefore, we do not know what he needs. If a man does not know what he is, how can he know what he should want?

Macmurray surveys modern thought from Descartes to the pre-

---

[4]Malcolm Muggeridge, *A Twentieth-Century Testimony* (Nashville: Thomas Nelson, 1979).

sent. The one great lack that he finds is an adequate model for our understanding of what constitutes a person.

Two models have been proposed. The first is a mechanical model. Drawn from the study of physics and mathematics, this model was of great help in explaining the material aspects of man. It permitted significant breakthroughs in physiology and various other fields of study. But when applied to an understanding of man as a self-determining, self-directing individual, the mechanical model proved inadequate. It could not explain the spontaneous, living, growing aspects of the human person. A larger model was necessary.

The second model of personhood is an organic model. As the first was drawn from the physical sciences, the second came from the biological. This model provided concepts that helped scientists deal with the processes of growth and biological change. But eventually it became obvious that the organic model did not do full justice to the personhood of man. The social scientist who embraced the organic model could not explain many facets of his own personality with it; so how could he explain the personalities of others? (Recall my budding sociologist friend. He found that in the existential decisions of life he could not make major choices without using concepts forbidden by his professional discipline, concepts that fall outside the purview of an organic model of man.)

The person to whom you preach is more complex than modern society thinks. The model of personhood used by psychologists, psychiatrists, journalists, leaders of government, and even by many leaders of the church is far too inadequate for its subject. A human being has fears, aspirations, and needs that even he—a child of this "enlightened" age—has not identified within himself. The cries of the self come up from within him like unknown tongues for which he has no interpreter. His sense of freedom and responsibility terrify him. The potential for both good and evil within point to mystery that at times borders on the ineffable. An Old Testament sage said that God has put eternity in our hearts; any model of personhood that is not open to the truth of eternity cannot explain man to himself. At this point the preacher who understands the truths of the Bible and who thinks in biblical categories can speak to human needs in a way that should make him the envy of every other professional counselor.

Where else will modern man find an adequate model for the self? He has looked around himself; it is not to be found there. Man must look above himself. The model is not in nature; it is in supernature. It is in the triune God whose image man bears.

It is no accident that the very word *person* entered our language from the Trinitarian discussions of the early church. The church fathers' attempt to explain the relationship of the Father, the Son, and the Spirit is what gave our world the very language of personhood. Why should it not also give us the model we are seeking? When the Western world retained the language of that debate but emptied the terms of their legitimate content, it set itself up for the crisis of modern thinking. Western men and women are masters of nature and of technology, but not of themselves. Because they no longer know God, they cannot know themselves.

The biblical model of the person is a far cry from the models proposed by modern man. It is far more complex and much richer. The biblical model of the person gives the lie to the modern illusion that man's fulfillment and true freedom are to be found in individualism and autonomy. This model reminds us that no person can be understood in isolation. Persons are not created that way. Even divine persons do not live that way.

Scripture and church tradition insist that God is three persons in one being. His unity is essential to his being. The three persons of the Godhead exist in differentiation and in relation with one another. The same is true of human persons. When you see one person, you know that he or she lives in relation with other persons. No person creates himself. For him to be, there had to be two parents in a relationship of love; his origin lay in that relationship. So to be a person is to be a social creature.

To be an isolated person is to be incomplete. In fact, if a perfect person were to be isolated, he would still be incomplete; even if he were a God-person, he would be incomplete. Such a person once walked this earth, and he said, "I can do nothing of myself. I can only do what I see the Father do. My Father has life in himself. He has given to me to have life in myself." And that person, Jesus Christ, is the model of our personhood. Isolated personhood by definition means incompleteness. Realization of that fact should dispel once and for all the myth of the self-sufficient individual who is "his own man" or "her own woman," who "stands on his (or her) own feet," who "does his (or her) own thing," and who is "responsible to no one." That is a myth and a delusion. Note these passages from the Gospel of John in which Jesus speaks of his relationship to the Father:

> ...I tell you the truth, the Son can do nothing by himself; he can do only what he sees his Father doing, because whatever the Father does the Son also does (5:19).

> For as the Father has life in himself, so he has granted the Son to have life in himself (5:26).

> All that the Father gives me will come to me, and whoever comes to me I will never drive away. For I have come down from heaven not to do my will but to do the will of him who sent me (6:37-38).

> Just as the living Father sent me and I live because of the Father, so the one who feeds on me will live because of me (6:57).

> ...I do nothing on my own but speak just what the Father has taught me. The one who sent me is with me; he has not left me alone, for I always do what pleases him (8:28-29).

The picture here is of a derived life, an other-oriented life. The second person of the Trinity draws his life from the first. He finds his fulfillment in submission to his Father, which means laying down his life for his friends. His fulfillment is not in doing his own will, in self-realization; it is in other directedness. In other words, his fulfillment is found in *love*. And his fulfillment is the model for ours.

Since every human being has a derived existence, we are neither self-originating, self-sustaining, nor self-fulfilling. Our origin, existence, and fulfillment are to be found through our relationship with an Other beyond ourselves. This is as true for the unbeliever as it is for the believer. Though the latter is more consciously aware of this relationship, and though the nature and extent of the believer's relationship are different, the personhood of the unbeliever is likewise rooted in his unconscious relationship with God. This has significant ramifications for our preaching. Only when we understand this fact will our preaching speak to the realities of those before us. Without understanding this, we will speak crudely and naively to the sort of people we think are there.

The Dynamics Of Receiving And Giving

Personal life is in essence a life of receiving and giving. (The order in which these two acts are mentioned is significant.) Nowhere are the effects of original sin more obvious than in man's refusal to accept this truth. We do not like the fact that life is a "given." We object to being grateful recipients. We think such an attitude obligates us to the giver, and we want neither to be dependent upon another nor responsible to another. We deny, defy, and resent the very idea of a dependent personal existence.

If we do not like to receive, we have equal difficulty in giving. We like to keep what we have. Yet life entangles us with spouses, children, relatives, friends, and others to whom we feel some obligation to give. So we give. Yet we tend to give with "hooks." We assume that our giving will obligate the recipient to return some favor to us. Gracious giving without expectation of return and without resentfulness are not easy. Unconditional love and unconditional giving are not natural for us in our sin.

The reality, though, is that nothing is more beautiful than gracious giving. We occasionally see it in human relationships. When we do, we laud it and call it sanctity (as with Mother Theresa of Calcutta). On the other hand, when we see a human relationship corrupted by someone's unwillingness to receive and give freely, we know that relationship has been defiled. We see that defilement in the parent who holds gifts over his children's heads until they respond to his generosity with the appropriate conduct. We see it in the wife who gives herself to the intimacy of marital sex only to get something that she wants from her husband. We see it in the friend who takes advantage of our friendship for personal gain. We are disappointed with such relationships. Love has become a barter and we know, whether or not we can say why, that such a perversion of the relationship is wrong. Persons are made supremely for love. That becomes clear when we recall our Model.

I remember a church leader and successful businessman who always gave me a suit for Christmas. As his pastor, I was grateful; but gradually I began to feel there were "hooks" in his giving, because he expected me to lend support to his projects in the church. I began to feel that I was being bought. So one Christmas I made sure that I was too busy to go with him to select the suit. That was the beginning of the end of my tenure in that pastorate!

No, it is not easy to receive and give freely. Yet every person cries for it. We were made for grace and love.

I heard a non-Christian once say of a Christian: "He did that for me at significant sacrifice to himself, when I knew I had nothing that he needed in return. I love him." We recognize gracious giving when we see it, and we are awed by the sight.

Thus, when we preach the grace, the love, and the unconditional mercy of Christ for the world, the message has an impact. The most self-centered sinner is thrown off guard by it. He finds the truth has a natural appeal. He was made for it. The word of his own nature and the word of grace are not antithetical; they reinforce one another.

We seem able to keep some receiving-giving relationships fairly clear. For example, I never resent one of my students who goes further in his academic achievements than I've gone; I can stand back and cheer him on. Lawyers are seldom jealous of doctors; preachers are never jealous of non-preachers. But lawyers can be fiercely jealous of other lawyers, and preachers envious of other preachers. What if we could be cleansed of that? What if we could find our supreme joy in giving encouragement to those who are laboring beside us?

We have the model for that sort of relationship in the Triune Godhead. The Father gives his life to the Son; the Son gives that life back to the Father; the two of them give their lives to the Spirit; and the Spirit glorifies the Father and the Son. That's the kind of receiving-giving relationship that every human being is made for; that's what eternity with God in the kingdom is going to be. Something within every person cries out for this sort of relationship. If we knew how to preach genuine personhood in those terms, and if we could make it clear, I think people would give their own invitation to accept Christ.

The Word of God in revelation and in nature are clearly related; we must be mindful of one if we are to understand the other. The creature without God has great possibilities—yet they remain unfulfilled until nature and grace touch each other.

5

The Law
Of The Second Witness

A source of great comfort to a preacher of God's Word is what I call the "'law of the second witness." It is an unfailing principle at work whenever the gospel is proclaimed: The preacher is never God's first witness in the hearer's life; God himself is already there before the preacher. The Holy Spirit has been at work in every person's life in numerous ways long before a preacher speaks the Word of truth to him. So the preacher never approaches someone "cold"; he can be sure that the Spirit of God is already at work in his hearer's life before the first word of his testimony is uttered or before the first point of his sermon is expounded.

This principle was dramatically illustrated for me on an airplane flight from Houston to San Antonio. Sitting next to me was a young man in an open shirt, intently reading and marking a history of Mexico. He was a handsome young man and I noticed that he had several maps of Mexico stacked on the seat between us. My curiosity was aroused. I thought that perhaps he was a missionary.

"Is that a good history of Mexico?" I asked.

"The best I've found," he replied, handing the book to me.

I leafed through the book and found that it was marked, much like a Ph.D. candidate's textbook would be marked for an oral exam. He had scribbled notes on all of the endpapers of the book. His handwriting was clear; his style was lucid; and not a word was misspelled. I perceived that he was well-educated. "Why are you interested in Mexico?" I inquired.

"I have a 30-day vacation and I want to see Mexico City and its environs on foot and by public transportation," he explained. That comment made me even more interested!

"What's your business?"

"I'm a high-school janitor." That made me much more interested! But at this point, my traveling companion asked what I was reading. I blushed, thinking, *This is sure to kill a conversation with a high-school janitor.* I handed him my copy of Saint Augustine's *Of the Trinity.* He took one look at it and asked, "Are you a Christian?"

"Yes. Are you a Christian?"

I expected him to say yes. But he replied, "Oh, no. I'm an atheist—at least I *think* I am."

That comment took me so much by surprise that I sat in silence for a moment. But the other fellow continued the conversation. He said, "Do you believe in prayer?"

"Yes, I do."

"'Why?"

At that time, we were experiencing the ordeal of Denny's hepatitis (described in chapter 3), so I related to my traveling companion how God was touching and healing our son. I finished telling about the miracle that had taken place in Denny's life by saying, "Yes! I believe in prayer."

My atheist friend looked at me and said, "That's wonderful. That's amazing. You know, I think I believe in prayer, too."

"Why?" I asked.

"Well,'" he said, "I had vicious migraine headaches that were destroying me. I went to every specialist that I thought could give me medical help and found no hope at all. The headaches were so unbearable that I decided I would commit suicide. But that made me think, *Religious people pray and they say that that helps sometimes. I don't suppose it would hurt me to try to pray. But how does* an atheist pray? I didn't know whether there was anyone to hear my prayer; or if there were someone, whether he would be interested in me; or if he were interested, whether he could help me or not. So I prayed: 'I don't know whether You are or not. I don't know whether You could or not. I don't know whether You would or not. But if You are and if You could and if You would, I would be most grateful.'

"The amazing thing is that the headaches went away. I thought, *What a lucky coincidence and what a happy one!* Then I had a second thought: *That's a cheap way out. What if there IS someone out there who is interested in me? What if there IS someone out there who did this and then I give credit to chance?* So I decided to pray again: 'I don't know whether You did or not; I don't even know whether You are or not. But if You are and You did, I want you to know my gratitude.'

"I had another thought," the atheist continued. "A lot of splendid serendipities have happened to me, things I never expected, things I never did anything to merit. They just dropped into my life—good things. So I thought, *What if there's somebody out there who cares about me enough that he did these things for me and I have taken them all for granted, never even stopping to say thank you?* So I prayed again: 'I don't know whether You did all those things or not; but if You did, I want You to know my gratitude.'"

I was very impressed by this, of course. My first thought was, *You may think you are an atheist; but you are a lot farther along than many of my Methodist friends.* But I said nothing. Suddenly he looked at me and said, "Do you think this conversation is an accident?"

I laughed and said, "No, I really don't. You see, I'm not even supposed to be on this plane. I had planned to be on another flight."

He laughed a little and said, "That's fascinating. I'm not supposed to be on this plane, either. When I got my ticket at the Braniff counter at O'Hare, the clerk told me that it was a non-stop flight from Chicago to Mexico City. And when I got on I found that it made two stops, one in Houston, one in San Antonio, before getting to Mexico City. I was mad as hops for an hour. But finally I decided that was no way to begin a vacation. You know, I don't believe this conversation is an accident."

At that point, the wheels of our plane hit the landing strip in San Antonio. When I felt the jar, I thought, *Lord, You can't let this conversation stop now. I've just gotten to the place where I can tell him about You.*

But I seemed to hear God's voice saying, "Well, I thought I was doing pretty well with him before you came along."

That experience has changed my attitude toward witnessing and preaching. I have come to realize that we are never first and we are never alone in witnessing. We never arrive in someone's life before the Holy Spirit. We never touch someone before God touches him. When God leads us to somebody, he has been there before us. We never preach to someone in whose life God has not already been at work. That prior work of the Spirit of grace makes the effectiveness of our witness possible. I call this "The Law of the Second Witness." Other theologians would call it prevenient grace. Recognition of this principle, no matter what we call it, can take a lot of burden and responsibility off of the preacher's back.

The Convicting Presence Of A Righteous God

Paul says that the law is our pedagogue to bring us to Christ. The law makes us guilty so that we feel our need of Christ; thus the law is an instrument of God's Spirit. Yet the law itself does not bring us deep guilt. The Holy Spirit does that. His divine presence quickens us in the presence of the law. We may have known that we had broken God's law and felt no soul-shaking guilt. But when the Holy Spirit enters our lives, we are suddenly smitten. Our guilt is no longer theoretical; it is now experiential. What makes the difference? God's presence. The Holy One has entered our lives.

This is illustrated by the experience of Peter, recorded in Luke 5. Jesus had used Peter's boat for a pulpit. Having finished his sermon, he sent Peter and his friends out into the deep and ordered them to cast their nets for fish. The catch was so large that the boat was filled with fish—enough to sink it. Peter fell down by the fish at the feet of Jesus and cried, "Go away from me, Lord; I am a sinful man" (v. 8).

What made Peter feel sinful? Not the unusual catch of fish, nor the danger of launching out into the deep. (Danger produces fear, not necessarily guilt.) No, it was the presence of Christ that made Peter conscious of his sin.

You and I may preach judgmentally and castigate our people; we may use our skills of exhortation and our biblical knowledge to try to produce guilt; but there is nothing redemptive in that. Through his Spirit, Christ produces the guilt that leads people to repentance. Things that caused them no great concern become unbearable burdens when he comes.[1]

Any attempt to manipulate or coerce our people in our own strength is sure to be deadly and counter-productive. Lasting spiritual fruit does not come from clever selection, of the "right" song, the telling of a dramatic story, or a display of emotion by the preacher to get the congregation to respond in the way he wants them to do. Granted, people will make a human response to an emotional human appeal. But eternal fruit comes when Christ is present in the service and when the pastor's witness matches that of the Spirit of God. Godly sorrow is vastly different from humanly evoked guilt.

Recall the incident in which the Pharisees brought a woman taken in adultery to Jesus. They were not mean enough to rejoice in the mere accomplishment of catching a woman in the act of adultery so they could put her on the spot. Undoubtedly, they wanted to test Jesus. But there may have been another factor at work: Perhaps these Pharisees were not bothered by guilt. Perhaps their lifestyle was so seriously religious that they felt morally superior to their fellow Jews. Until they met Jesus! Something about him broke

---

[1] For this reason, most people come to conversion or to holiness of heart out of a crisis in which they realize their own defeat and inadequacy.

through their religious facade and threatened their smugness. Perhaps they were pleased to bring the adulteress to Jesus because she made them look better by comparison. At least they did not practice adultery!

That is how most of us handle guilt. We try to find someone who looks guiltier than we do; we compare ourselves with those who seem morally inferior. We can always manage to find such people.

Jesus did not deny the reality of the woman's sin. He simply forced the Pharisees' attention back to their relationship to him: "If any one of you is without sin, let him be the first to throw a stone at her" (John 8:7). Jesus would not let them dwell on her sinfulness; he forced them to consider their own. And from the oldest to the youngest, they realized their own sin and began to slip away.

In his presence we cannot avoid ourselves by looking at others. Jesus forces us to compare ourselves with him. His presence brings us to confess our guilt, not to moralize about the guilt of others.

We preachers should work with him in this process. When the Word is preached and Christ is present, when the preacher's word confirms what Christ is already saying to the sinner, the results can be revolutionary. There is power when the two witnesses converge. The preacher should never forget, though, which witness comes first.

Practical Implications
For The Preacher's Preparation

How should all of this affect the preacher's mental and spiritual preparation before he steps into the pulpit on a given Sunday? How, in practical terms, does recognition of the Holy Spirit's prior work affect what the preacher does?

It ought to mean that the preacher is continually trying to read the mind of the Spirit in terms of his congregation; he should try to discern, by virtue of the Holy Spirit's revelation, where they are and where God is trying to take them next. He can do that only if his private life is open to God and his public life is open to his people. This is why I think pastoral visitation is so important. This is why it's important for us to keep abreast of what's happening in the culture around us. We should know something of what is being fed into the minds of the people to whom we are preaching. We should know the concerns and the interests of our people. We must be in this kind of dialogue with our people. Through personal prayer, Bible study, and private worship, we must be in dialogue with the Holy Spirit. We must sense the configuration of God's work among our people and then attempt to fit into the divine pattern.

The law of the second witness should also affect a preacher's attitude toward "disruptions" in his personal life and in the life of his congregation. All of us have been irritated by occurrences that seem to be demonically designed to disturb our peace of mind and upset our program of life. But we must remember that God is sovereign; nothing happens in our lives without his consent. Therefore we should look carefully at annoyances to see if we can discern God's hand at work.

Mark 1 records a situation in which Jesus was disturbed in the midst of his lesson by a demoniac. Yet that disturbance provided an occasion for Jesus to show his authority over all evil. The lowering of the paralytic through the roof (Mark 2) did not enhance Jesus' sermon; but it did give him an opportunity to show his power to restore physical health, as well as his right to forgive sins. No one remembers Jesus' sermon that day. We remember something better!

If we believe that Jesus is at work in the congregation before we are, if we believe he is more actively committed to reaching his people than we are, then we will keep our eyes open to his activity in the "disturbances" and the "annoyances" that come our way, so that we can work with him. Often what appears to be an unfortunate accident proves to be a clue to the workings of the Lord.

This necessitates a higher view of the sovereignty of God than some of us have maintained. God's sovereignty does not mean that we should passively abdicate our responsibility for planning and decision-making. We dare not be simply submissive to circumstances. But it does mean that we live with our eyes open to the opportunities God will provide unexpectedly.

The law of the second witness should affect every aspect of worship planning. Even in the smallest church that is least interested in worship forms, the pastor should plan every worship service with great care. He should do some specific things to help create an atmosphere in which the Spirit can work best, since the Spirit's inner witness is of prior importance to the preacher's witness of the spoken word.

First, be sure there is an integrity to the service. Choose hymns to fit the message that you intend to bring; this cannot be done haphazardly. If you are to give the Holy Spirit maximum opportunity, you must be quite familiar with your hymnal! Your hymns, Scripture readings, and sermon should harmoniously complement each other.

Second, be sensitive to the fact that the commonplace is difficult to bring to life. Familiar Scripture passages may be the hardest passages to expound because you think you know them, just as your people think they do.

Likewise you may find it very hard to use gospel songs to create an atmosphere of worship because most people sing them by rote, without thinking.[2] Thus a hymn, with its fuller statement of biblical truth, has more enduring usefulness. Even the unfamiliar hymn, if properly introduced, can be a special instrument of the Spirit. The unfamiliar should not be sung for the sake of mere novelty, of course; everything in the service should point the congregation to what you believe God wishes to say to his people in that hour.

A new expression of an old and familiar truth can have profound power. I thought I knew every invitation hymn used by evangelical churches until I found myself singing for the first time Gerhard Tersteegen's "God Calling Yet." The form and style of the hymn were not what I expected to conclude an evangelistic service. But I found myself deeply moved as I sang:

---

[2]The glory of the gospel song is also its weakness. Simplicity and repetition make the gospel song an effective tool for evangelism until it becomes so commonplace that no one needs to think what he is singing.

God calling yet; shall I not hear?
Earth's pleasures, shall I still hold dear?
Shall life's swift passing years all fly,
And still my soul in slumber lie?

God calling yet; shall I not rise?
Can I His longing voice despise,
And basely His kind care repay?
He calls me still; can I delay?

God calling yet; and shall He knock,
And I my heart the closer lock?
He still is waiting to receive,
And shall I dare His Spirit grieve?

God calling yet; I cannot stay;
My heart I yield without delay;
Vain world, farewell! from thee I part;
The voice of God has reached my heart.

—Gerhard Tersteegen

My inner response was startling. I suddenly became aware of the pull of earth's pleasures. The danger to a soul asleep in its sins moved clearly into view. The tender call of the loving Savior resounded in my heart. The real possibility of grieving his Spirit shook my soul. I wanted no sins or weights to numb me; I wanted to "yield without delay" to his voice. I wanted all those around me to hear the voice that had spoken to my own heart. And more, I wanted to share that hymn with my people when I returned home!

New expressions of old truth can make the familiar live with power again; so do not neglect to introduce new hymns to your people.

Third, give attention to details, for even the smallest aspects of the worship service can make an important difference in your preparation for the Spirit's work. The Scripture passages should be read with as much care as led to their selection. Scripture should be read beforehand so that the reader can give it proper cadence and emphasis; in this way, the listener clearly hears the message of the Scripture and gains some indication of the thrust of the passage.

Prepare for the public prayer with equal thoughtfulness. This does not mean you should read the prayer. But you should avoid surrendering these meaningful moments of the service to capricious inspiration *ex tempore*. If one knew he had five minutes to state a crucial case before a judge, he would weigh carefully what he wanted to say. No one should give less thought to speaking to the sovereign Lord than he would to the earth's highest potentate.

Special music should be as much a part of the message of the hour. Everything to be included in the worship service should be tested against these questions: *Will it help to convey the message of the Lord to his people? And will it give the Holy Spirit the freedom he needs to work?* For these things to be so, the service should be planned as an integrated whole.

Fourth, provide for an appropriate use of silence in the worship service. We often sing,

> The Lord is in his holy temple:
>   let all the earth keep silence before him (Hab. 2:20 KJV).

Though we sing about silence, we give little place for it in our worship services. We could learn much from our Quaker friends at this point; they have understood the use of silence far better than we have. If we really believe that the Lord is present and is the primary witness in the worship service, let us give him more opportunity to have our undivided attention. Let us provide some moments for "the still small voice" of God to speak to our souls.

Silence may be of value at any point in the service. It may be especially significant at the end, when the congregation is allowed to think about what has been said, listening for the inner voice of God's Holy Spirit and choosing to take some initial steps of commitment to him.

An English friend of mine employed silence in a most unique way to seek commitments from his congregation. At the close of a worship service, he would ask for a time of silence while the congregation bowed their heads. After an appropriate pause, he would say, "If God is speaking to you and you want to seal your response to what he is saying, just lift your head and look at me. I will see you." The atmosphere would become almost electric with a sense of God's presence. Those who raised their heads and opened their eyes confirmed a covenant with God, their pastor being a witness to it. Needless to say, this simple expression of commitment had a liberating effect on many who responded. As someone has said, "Impression without expression means depression. With expression, it becomes liberation."

Such moments of silence at the end of a service will turn people's attention from the written Word to the living Word within. Silence reminds the congregation that their response to God should be personal and active, not just cognitive.

If the foregoing paragraphs express your philosophy of worship, it should not be necessary for me to underscore the importance of praying before the service that the double witness will be at work. Prayer opens the channels through which the Spirit of God comes. Prayer makes us sensitive to his presence. Why should he come when we are not ready to receive him? And how can we perceive what he is saying if he does not have our attention?

An automobile salesman said to his pastor, "Your job is easy. When a customer comes into our showroom, I have to convince him he needs a new car; I have to convince him he needs one of mine; I have to convince him he can pay for it; and I have to convince him he ought to take it now. And I have to do it all by myself. But," he said, "you stand up there and all the time you are preaching, the Holy Ghost in my heart is saying, 'You know he's right. You know you ought to respond.'"

Prayer can prepare the way for the Spirit's coming. He is more eager to come than we are to have him come. He is the one who stands and knocks at our heart-door first. But if we prepare our hearts in prayer, we will find the reliability of Jesus' promise: "For where two or three come together in my name, there am I with them" (Matt. 18:20). It does not matter whether the congregation

6

The Essential Relationship

If a preacher is to be a true messenger of God, he must have the Holy Spirit in his life. The Old Testament lays the groundwork for such an understanding. Each major office in the life of Israel was to be filled by someone anointed by the Holy Spirit. The priest and the king always (and the prophet on occasion) began their work by being anointed with olive oil, which was symbolic of the Spirit of God. What qualified a Saul or a David to be king in Israel? Not their possession of the crown or the throne, nor a royal lineage; it was their anointing by God. The king of Israel was not considered to be an autonomous ruler. He had to be under divine control in order to qualify to reign over his people. Note that when Saul insisted upon doing things in his own way, for example, the Holy Spirit departed from him and came upon David. Saul still had the crown, the throne, the bodyguard, and the palace; but David had the anointing of God. Even while hiding in the cave in fear of his life, David was the regal one. This may be why David prayed in Psalm 51:11,

> Do not cast me from your presence,
> or take your Holy Spirit from me.

He clearly remembered the tragedy of King Saul, who lost the true kingship even though he retained all of its symbols. David did not want to spend his life that way. His personal gifts were of importance; but the divine anointing made him the true king.

That same anointing was required for the priest and the prophet. The heart of the consecration of the priest was an anointing with oil, symbolically representing the Holy Spirit. The story of Moses and the seventy (Num. 11) and Elisha's desire for a double portion of the Spirit that was on Elijah (2 Kings 2:9) illustrate the Old Testament identification of true prophecy with the anointing of the Spirit. No man was to stand in God's stead alone; he must have the power of the Spirit if he was to lead God's people aright.

The New Testament picks up this theme and amplifies it. Before he left his disciples, Jesus insisted that they not depart Jerusalem until they received divine preparation for their ministry by receiving the Holy Spirit. In his own life, Jesus set the pattern for all of us who are in ministry. Though he was the eternal Son of God, the second person of the Trinity, he began his ministry after receiving the Spirit; all four of the Gospels record that event (Matt. 3:13-17; Mark 1:9-11; Luke 3:21-22; John 1:29-34). He was not ready to begin his redemptive messianic ministry without that anointing. In fact, the anointing of the Spirit was definitive of his character and role. The very word *Christ* (Gk., Χριστόσ) or *Messiah* means "the anointed One."

The importance of this emerges clearly in his interaction with the Pharisees (Matt. 12:22ff.; Luke 11:14ff.). Disturbed by Christ and hostile to him, the Pharisees try to explain his power as of demonic origin. He assures them that the source of his power is not the Devil, but the Holy Spirit:

> ....If I drive out demons by the Spirit of God, then the kingdom of God has come upon you (Matt. 12:28).

How significant that the Christ does his work in the power of the Spirit! By virtue of that fact, he can call us to do his work: "As my Father has sent me so send I you," he said. We are to finish his work; and to finish his work we need the same anointing that he had. When he says, "Greater works than these shall he do" (John

14:12 KJV), we can be quite certain that they will be done only by the same Spirit that resided upon him.

The Spirit As Source

Those who carefully read the Gospels will understand why a Christian minister needs the presence and power of the Holy Spirit. The teachings in the Gospel of John concerning the Holy Spirit vividly illustrate this. Perhaps the definitive text for all ministry is John 6:63, in which Jesus says, "The Spirit gives life; the flesh counts for nothing." This sums up the biblical teaching that the life our people need cannot come from us but is given only by the Spirit.

John 3 describes Jesus' interview with Nicodemus, an expert in the religion of Israel. Jesus tells him of a source from beyond himself, the Spirit of God; the Spirit gives new life. A preacher who proclaims the kingdom of God must rely on the same source. All that the preacher desires to achieve depends totally upon the Holy Spirit and can be done only by the Spirit.

In a sense, the preacher plays a role in redemption that is analogical to that of the midwife or obstetrician. As an attendant at birth, he has the power to help or hinder that birth. A doctor once said to me, "The beauty of a natural birth is that there is so little a physician can do to interfere." We do have the power, however, as yielded instruments of God and co-workers with God, to help create the context in which the Spirit can bring forth new offspring for the kingdom. This process is a mystery, as Jesus indicated to Nicodemus; but it is a mystery into which God would induct his own servants.

The Spirit is the source of spiritual life, first of all. Secondly, he is the source of spiritual overflow. That is apparent in John 7:37-39, where Jesus says,

> 'If anyone is thirsty, let him come to me and drink. Whoever believes in me, as the Scripture has said, streams of living water will flow from within him.' By this he meant the Spirit, whom those who believed in him were later to receive. Up

to that time the Spirit had not been given, since Jesus had not yet been glorified.

While Jesus emphasized the Spirit's *inflow* in John 3, he emphasizes the Spirit's *outflow* in John 7. It is safe to say that in John 7 he is thinking about ministry rather than life. He teaches that there should be such a working of the Spirit within the minister's life that it provides a spiritual overflow for those who are around him. In fact, this is the reason every Christian should be filled with the Spirit—so that he has not only grace for his own needs but an overflowing grace for others.

Ezekiel 47 presents an intriguing vision of a stream that flows out of the temple of God. The miraculous stream has no augmentation—no tributaries contribute to it—nonetheless it grows and brings life everywhere it goes. Where there has been death, it brings resurrection; where there has been sterility, it brings fruit; where there has been putrefaction, it brings healing. Now what is the temple? It is your heart and mine. Every Christian is the temple of the Holy Spirit.[1] I think the fountain of John 7 and the stream of Ezekiel 47 are parables of what every Christians ministry should be.

The temple was built on a mount of solid rock and there was never any water in the temple naturally; it had to be carried in. This makes the symbolism of Ezekiel 47 and John 7 all the more dramatic. Note B. F. Wescott's comment on John 7:37-38:

> 'And on that last day, the great day of the feast, Jesus stood and cried, saying: If a man thirst and come unto me…from out of his inward parts will flow rivers of living water.' The image of 'if a man thirst' appears to have been occasioned by the libations of water brought in a golden vessel from Siloam, which were made at the time of the morning sacrifice on each of the seven days of the feast while Isaiah 12:3 was sung. It is uncertain whether the libations were made on the eighth day. If they were not made, the significant cessation of the striking

---

[1] In a very real sense, the preacher ought to be preeminently a temple of the Spirit. The great pastors have always been temples of God's Spirit. Out of their lives have flowed a life-giving stream that brought life and fruitfulness to other people.

rite on this day of the feast would give us a still more fitting occasion for the words.

The pouring out of the water was a commemoration of one conspicuous detail of the life in the wilderness typified by the festival. The water brought from the rocks implied an image of future blessing to the prophets (Ezek. 47:1-12). That gift is definitely connected with the Lord by St. Paul in 1 Corinthians 10:4. Christ therefore shows how the promise of those early miracles was completely fulfilled in himself in a higher form. He who drank of that water thirsted again, but the water of which Christ gave became a spring of water within.[2]

That provision is for us, but Christ cannot give it to us until we see our need for it. A study of Christian biography reveals that it is not unusual for a person to live as a Christian for several years before he senses from his own experience and realizes from reading Scripture the difference between a life "born of the Spirit" and one that "overflows with the Spirit." A good illustration of this is found in the testimony of Samuel Chadwick, one of the great Methodist preachers of Great Britain in the nineteenth century and the principal of Cliff College:

While he was a young pastor, a prayer league had been formed in his congregation. Every week the members met at the house of a godly leader of the church. Every member of the league received a little notebook in which were written the names of those who entered into this fellowship of intercession. The only rules were that each member should pray every day for revival and that they should meet together for united prayer once a week.

Praying for the conversion of others, the young pastor turned the searchlight to his own heart. He saw his need of cleansing and of enduement of power. The crisis narrowed down to a conflict of wills: God required and he demurred. It was not that he was conscious of any sin in his life; as often happens,

---

[2]B. F. Westcott, *The Gospel According to John* (Grand Rapids: William B. Eerdmans, 1951), p. 123.

the very thing he had consecrated to God was the cause of the struggle. He believed himself called to preach. He prided himself upon his sermons. He had no desire to be an evangelist, but with marvelous industry he had spent many hours snatched from sleep in careful construction of his sermons and in search of illustrations. He came to Stacksteeds parish with 15 sermons of which he was proud and he believed the preaching of them would bring a revival of religion. He preached a dozen of them and the revival still tarried, nor was his own soul at peace.

It was Saturday night. His thoughts were on the morrow. He was going over his notes for the last time. God put his finger on the sermons and the young preacher understood. He had believed his strength was in these sermons and had forgotten that God alone is able to save. There was a struggle. It went on through the midnight hour. At 3:00 on Sunday morning, a fire was kindled in the kitchen grate and the sermons were burned. The blessing had come.

The work of converting grace began that day. At the early morning prayer meeting, he witnessed to an experience of sanctification and led his first convert to Jesus. Before the day closed, 7 people were converted and, as he used to say, God gave him one for every barren year of his preaching. He called for a week of prayer in the church, suspending the ordinary meetings. The attendance grew night by night. The meetings went on into the second week and the area of the chapel filled.

On Thursday night, something happened. Two leaders were present who were always at variance. Temperamentally they were uncongenial; socially they were rivals. During the meeting, one of them got up and quietly came and knelt at the communion rail. Then the other came and knelt at her side. Hand in hand, first one prayed and then the other. Others came and knelt beside them. There was no rant but a subdued sense of repentance and assured confidence that Christ was there.[3]

[3]Norman G. Dunning, *Samuel Chadwick* (London: Hodder and Stoughton Ltd., 1933), pp. 42-44.

THE ESSENTIAL RELATIONSHIP   99

That was the first time Samuel Chadwick had seen Pentecost come to a praying people. He was in revival. Out of that came the conversion of the most notorious drunkard in the town and the beginning of a movement of the Spirit that led to the conversion of many people.

The pattern of Chadwick's experience fits what Jesus promised in the Gospel of John. Without question he had experienced the new birth—the tenor of his life gave evidence of that—and he had been clearly called to preach. But a fruitful ministry was lacking because he relied upon his own ability and his own working. That self-dependence was not the result of willful disobedience to God; Chadwick simply had not allowed the Spirit of God to work fully and freely through him. His sermons symbolized his self-dependence. They were his crutches—and crutches can become idols. The night the Holy Spirit moved upon his heart, Chadwick burned the sermons that were his idol and crutch, and God was able to use him effectively. A life that God had entered was now one that he filled. A similar experience can be identified in the lives of men like R. A. Torrey, Dwight L. Moody, and most of the great soulwinners in the English-speaking world.

The Holy Spirit obviously works with more freedom through some preachers than he does through others. I attribute this in part to the sovereign character of his working. The Spirit works as he wills and uses whom he chooses. This is evidenced by the fact that he works differently at different times *in the same person's life,* irrespective of any spiritual change. The question should not be whether he is free to use another person more than he uses you or me, but whether he is as free to use you and me as he desires. Are the hindrances gone from our lives? Are we free channels of his grace? If not, how do we become free channels? More on that later.

The Spirit In Ministry

The third portion of teaching about the person and work of the Spirit in the Gospel of John is found in chapters 14-16. In chapter 3, Jesus spoke to a Jew about new life. In chapter 7, he preached to a temple of dry and lifeless religious people about overflow. Now in the privacy of the Upper Room, he speaks to the disciples about their need of the Holy Spirit.

These were very tender moments. In a few hours Jesus would be on the cross. In a few days the resurrection and the ascension will have taken place. The disciples will remain in the world to finish the work he began; thus they will need his power to do his work. So he speaks to them of the Holy Spirit.

First, Jesus explains who the Holy Spirit is. He is another Counselor who will take Christ's place in their lives (John 14:16). What Jesus has been to them for three years, now the Holy Spirit will become. The word used for *another* (Gk., ἄλλον) literally means "another of the same kind." And this Counselor will not be taken from them; he is to remain with them forever.

The Holy Spirit is to be their Teacher (John 14:25-26). As Jesus has instructed them in spiritual matters and in the practice of ministry, now the Spirit will teach them. He will remind them of all Christ has said. As they face new and unexpected situations, he will guide them. He will not speak of himself, but of Christ (15:26-27). The Spirit's own emphasis upon Christ will remind the disciples that they are to be witnesses of Christ, who sends them into the world, as Christ was the witness of the Father who sent him. As they witness about Christ in the power of the Spirit, the Spirit will bear witness to the testimony that the disciples give. The Holy Spirit and the disciples will be co-witnesses of Jesus Christ.

Further, Jesus says, the Spirit will convince and convict the world (16:7-11). The disciples are not to be the prosecutors of sinners; the Holy Spirit will do that. He will make men's consciences come alive to their sin. He will sensitize their spirits to true righteousness. He will open their eyes to see the consequences of their sin and unbelief.

Finally, the Holy Spirit will be the medium through whom all that the Father has shared with the Son will become the possession of the believer (16:13-15). Jesus said, "All that belongs to the Father is mine...." Now the Spirit takes that which the Father has given to the Son and gives it to the disciples.

He is Teacher, Fellow-Witness, Mediator between the believer and Christ. This is why John Taylor refers to the Holy Spirit as "the go-between God." Little wonder that on Easter Sunday evening Jesus, in his first appearance to his disciples after the resurrection, says, "Receive the Holy Spirit" (John 20:22b). And on the Mount of Ascension, he says to all gathered there,

> Do not leave Jerusalem, but wait for the gift my Father promised, which you have heard me speak about.... In a few days you will be baptized with the Holy Spirit (Acts 1:4b-5).

If the Holy Spirit is the *sine qua non* of spiritual life, he is equally essential to doing the work Christ sent his disciples to do.

But our natural tendency is to hinder the Spirit. We need to have our wills purified and fixed on him so that we do not obstruct his working through us. Purity of will comes only as the Holy Spirit imparts his life to us in fullness.

A minister should share love with a needy world; but it is Christ's love that must be shared, the love that only the Holy Spirit can shed abroad in our hearts. A. B. Simpson says simply, "We are the capacity. He is the supply."

The Spirit Transforms Ordinary People

When a person surrenders to the Holy Spirit, the consequences are always significant. Often it seems as if the Spirit takes special pleasure in using those who, apart from the Spirit's anointing, would be poorly qualified. He does the unexpected with the ordinary. This is especially obvious in periods of revival.

During the 1970 revival at Asbury College, churches invited students, staff, and faculty to come and share the news of what God was doing. As they went, their simple telling of the story almost inevitably reproduced in some measure what had happened at Asbury. The impressiveness or gifts of the person telling the story had little to do with the results. The following incident will show what I mean:

Dr. Donald Irwin, pastor of the college church at Olivet Nazarene College in Kankakee, Illinois, was preparing to enter the Saturday night service of a weekend revival when his head usher told him two students from Asbury College wanted to see him. Noting that he still had ten minutes before the service was to begin, Dr. Irwin told the usher he could bring them in.

Two very ordinary-looking young men strode into his study. They told the pastor that revival had broken out at Asbury, that many people who had never known God were finding him, and that Christians were finding him in a more powerful way. These two fellows had been praying together the night before, when God told them they should visit Olivet College and share with the students what God was doing at Asbury.

Dr. Irwin expressed his delight at the news, but indicated that he could not invite them to speak from the pulpit of the church because they were strangers to him. Their response surprised him. They said, "No problem! God told us to come. We've obeyed him. So everything's fine." Dr. Irwin sensed no negative feelings on their part as he turned them away and they started down the hall.

Dr. Irwin's own spirit checked him. He found himself calling, "Wait a minute, fellows. Come back. How long will it take you to share your story? Could you do it in five minutes, after the first hymn?"

They assured him they could do it in less time, if he desired. They just wanted to be obedient to the Holy Spirit.

So after the opening hymn, Dr. Irwin briefly introduced the two students. The first stood and simply told who he was and how God was at work in Asbury College. He indicated that many people were finding God, torn relationships were being repaired, lives were being transformed, and the Lord had told them to come and share the news. He sat down and the second student arose and said about the same thing. The two young men took no more than four minutes to tell their story, and there was no noticeable response from the crowd. Dr. Irwin announced that a quartet would sing next.

The quartet finished their first verse. Before they could begin the second, their bass went to the altar, sobbing. Twelve to fifteen other people rose from various places in the auditorium and came to the altar.

The service was being broadcast by radio. Many who listened felt the tug of God at their hearts, left what they were doing, and drove to the church. By nine o'clock there were more people in the sanctuary than when the service began. Many who came did not stop to take a seat but went directly to the altar to make their peace with God.

The next morning, about twenty carloads of students drove from Olivet to churches and colleges around the country to tell about the revival. Wherever they went, the Spirit attended their witness as he had that of the two students the night before.

When the Spirit can get a channel, the channel does not count as much as the Spirit.

The Spirit is the key to effective witness; but he is also the key to holy living. When the Spirit fills us, he cleanses us too. He makes as much difference in our living as in our serving. Another story from the life of Samuel Chadwick illustrates this. We were privileged to have visiting in our home a British evangelist who had been a student at Cliff College when Chadwick was the principal there. Since Chadwick's writings on prayer and the work of the Holy Spirit had deeply impressed me, I asked our visitor to tell what sort of person Chadwick was. This is the story he told:

No guest speaker was scheduled in the Thursday chapel services at Cliff College; instead the students and staff were invited to share their prayer requests, testimonies, and prayers of intercession. In one of these services, a student arose and told how he was fighting an unexpected battle with jealousy. He asked everyone to pray for him. Dr. Chadwick listened sympathetically and then recounted an experience with jealousy from his own life.

Chadwick had received an invitation to be one of two Bible

teachers at a well-known conference in Britain. The other speaker was to be G. Campbell Morgan. Chadwick said, "It did not really hurt my pride to be invited to work with Morgan, since at that time he was easily the best-known preacher in the English language. I thought, *What an honor to be speaking on the same program with G. Campbell Morgan! Perhaps some folks are taking notice of me!*"

Chadwick prepared carefully for the conference. He was mindful of the fact that he and Morgan were to speak at successive hours and were to alternate times every other day.

The first morning Chadwick spoke to a large crowd in the first hour and Morgan spoke to a comparable crowd for the second. The next morning Morgan spoke to a large crowd in the first service. But when Chadwick arose to speak, great numbers of people left. The next morning Chadwick spoke to a small group first; then a large audience came in for Morgan.

Chadwick was hurt. He went to his room and knelt in prayer. "This is not fair, Lord," he said.

"Oh?" the Lord seemed to reply. "What do you want me to do about this?"

"Well, I don't know. But it hurts. It's embarrassing."

Chadwick was not prepared for the Lord's response: "Are you sorry, Chadwick, that we've got a fellow like Morgan on our team?"

"No!" Chadwick replied. "But it hurts."

"Are you suggesting that I quit blessing Morgan?" the Lord continued.

Then Chadwick saw the truth. He found himself saying, "Forgive my attitude, Lord. No, I am not sorry we've got a fellow like this on our team, and I don't want you to quit blessing him.'"

That day and for the rest of the conference, Samuel Chadwick blocked out a time to pray for G. Campbell Morgan and for the success of his ministry. Chadwick said, "After that I found myself going with excitement to hear Morgan each day, giving thanks that we had a fellow like that on our team." Morgan's success was now Chadwick's success because both of them were working with the same Spirit. It seems to me that this is illustrative of what Paul means when he says, "...All things are yours, whether Paul or Apollos or Cephas or the world or life or death or the present or the future—all are yours, and you are of Christ, and Christ is of God" (1 Cor. 3:21-23).

When the Spirit comes in his sanctifying fullness, he cleanses us of the self-interest that corrupts all we touch apart from his cleansing. He sets us free to rejoice in his work, not in ours. In fact, we find true fulfillment only in his working, no matter how or through whom he comes. This is the real liberation of Christian living, liberation from the inward bonds of self.

Christ And His Spirit
Our Central Concern

If the work we cry to see done is Christ's work and if he alone can do it, then his freedom to work through us is our top priority. He becomes central in our concern, even more central than the work we are called to do. This should not surprise us. If Christ wills to do his work in this world through us, then our cooperation and submission to him is crucial, and resistance is our greatest sin. Anything that hinders Christ from working through us is a frustration of our own deepest purposes.

Here we come face-to-face with our (and his) greatest enemy, the carnal self-will. We know Christ and love him. But we find an inner recalcitrance, an unwillingness to say a total yes to the One we love and serve. We desire to keep some semblance of control over our lives. We are unable to abdicate that control, even to the One we love and want to serve. No preacher has faced the loving claims of the Holy Spirit, as He seeks to make him a clean channel and joyous co-worker with Christ, without sensing his own will to resist even the One he loves.

Usually we must walk with Christ for awhile before we realize the measure of our refractoriness. The cleverness and cunning of the ego are such, as it seeks to maintain its own autonomy, that it can claim to be surrendering to Christ while it keeps its hand on the controls. True surrender is never a noble gesture; it is the capitulation of a rebel, no matter how much the unsanctified ego would like to make it look otherwise. But the recognition of our own recalcitrance is the first step toward a Spirit-filled and Spirit-anointed life. George Matheson understood this; notice the verbs in his great hymn:

> Make me a captive, Lord,
>   And then I shall be free;
> Force me to render up my sword,
>   And I shall conqueror be.
> I sink in life's alarms
>   When by myself I stand;
> Imprison me within Thine arms,
>   And strong shall be my hand.
>
> My heart is weak and poor
>   Until it master find;
> It has no spring of action sure,
>   It varies with the wind.
> It cannot freely move
>   Till Thou hast wrought its chain;
> Enslave it with Thy matchless love,
>   And deathless it shall reign.
>
> My power is faint and low
>   Till I have learned to serve;
> It wants the needed fire to glow,
>   It wants the breeze to nerve;
> It cannot drive the world
>   Until itself be driven;
> Its flag can only be unfurled
>   When Thou shalt breathe from heaven.
>
> My will is not my own
>   Till Thou hast made it Thine;
> If it would reach a monarch's throne,
>   It must its crown resign.
> It only stands unbent
>   Amid the clashing strife,
> When on Thy bosom it has leant,
>   And found in Thee its life.

You will note that all the verbs in that first verse are imperatives as Matheson prays to become wholly the Lord's. The verbs *make, force, imprison,* and *enslave* all speak of a heart that now sees its basic sinfulness, its inability to trust its Love. That is the believer's great dilemma.

Matheson like Wesley saw that salvation from self-centeredness is as much of God's grace as is the forgiveness of sins. He saw that the greater bondage is not to sin but to an uncleansed self, turned in upon itself. His heart cries for true and full freedom, the freedom of the sons of God. Whence shall that freedom come? He knows it can come only from God. Note again the lines about the self:

> It cannot drive the world
> Until itself be driven;
> Its flag can only be unfurled
> When Thou shalt breathe from heaven.

Freedom to surrender wholly to the One we love comes only when the divine Spirit blows in cleansing, freeing power upon us just as he did upon the 120 disciples at Pentecost. Edwin Hatch seems to echo Matheson's prayer in his great hymn:

> Breathe on me, Breath of God,
> Fill me with life anew,
> That I may love what Thou dost love,
> And do what Thou wouldst do.
>
> Breathe on me, Breath of God,
> Until my heart is pure.
> Until with Thee I will one will,
> To do and to endure.
>
> Breathe on me, Breath of God,
> Till I am wholly Thine,
> Until this earthly part of me
> Glows with Thy fire divine.
>
> Breathe on me, Breath of God,
> So shall I never die,
> But live with Thee the perfect life
> Of Thine eternity.

You will observe Hatch's concern. He wants to love what God loves and do what God would do. He wants his will to become one with God's so that he can wholly belong to God. It is significant that he turns now, not to the Father nor to the Son, but to the Holy Spirit and pleads for the "Breath of God" to "breathe from heaven," purifying him until every earthly part of his life "'glows with Thy fire divine."

The demands of Christian ministry are radical. The needs of our hearts are radical. The divine provision for us is equally radical: the very Spirit who anointed and filled Jesus the Christ. God's work can be done only by God, but he needs what Simpson called "empty possibilities" through whom he can work. How do we become that?

How To Be Filled
With The Holy Spirit

First, we must recognize our need. Usually this becomes clear as we walk with the Lord long enough to see our inadequacies and our sinfulness. There may be exceptions to this pattern; but most of us are like Chadwick. Amid our struggle to please Christ, we realize that we tend to rely upon ourselves and serve Christ in our own strength. Then the reality of life and the Spirit himself expose us to ourselves. We see our inner recalcitrance. Then the Spirit's cleansing fullness becomes a *necessity,* not a luxury. (God is never a luxury!)

So first we must see our need of the Spirit's infilling. As long as we think there is some other way to serve God acceptably, he will let us try it.

Second, we must believe that the Holy Spirit not only *can* fill and cleanse our spirits, but *will.* If there is any question in our minds about either his ability or his willingness, we will falter in our asking. Faith is the condition for the Holy Spirit to do his work in our hearts. We must believe the Spirit will do what Jesus promised.

Peter recognized this in reporting to the Jerusalem Council what happened at Cornelius' house:

> God, who knows the heart, showed that he accepted them by giving the Holy Spirit to them, just as he did to us. He made no distinction between us and them, for he purified their hearts by faith (Acts 15:8-9).

God is more eager to give his Spirit in fullness than we are to receive him. Note Luke 11:13:

> If you then, though you are evil, know how to give good gifts to your children, how much more will your Father in heaven give the Holy Spirit to those who ask him!

Note also the urgency with which Jesus insisted that his disciples not leave Jerusalem until they had received the promised gift of the Father, the Holy Spirit (Acts 1:4b-5). God made us to be his temples; it is his will to fill us.

Third, we must be willing for him to fill and possess us. If we insist upon keeping our hands upon our lives, even occasionally, this insistence will hinder him. This does not mean that we must joyously and freely surrender ourselves to the Holy Spirit before we can enjoy his fullness; that would be underestimating the human lust for autonomy. A person does not easily die to self-control and sinful self-interest. One cannot crucify himself; Christ must crucify him. But if Christ is to put the spikes in the self, we must be ready to consent—no matter how awkwardly. At this point we discover how double-dealing the self can be. One part of the self cries out to be possessed by God; yet another part resists. We must tell Christ which "I" within us we choose to let speak on our behalf.

The beauty is that the very Christ into whom we put the nails can now put his spike into us. We imposed our spikes upon him; but his consent to that imposition now allows him to conquer us through his Spirit.

Fourth, we must trust the Spirit to fill us now. Charles Inwood, a British Methodist and world-renowned Keswick speaker, tells how he came to this realization. Inwood was converted as a lad. The assurance of salvation refreshed his spirit and he walked joyfully with Christ. God called him to preach and he entered the ministry.

But as he preached, he felt a great hunger of soul, a deep desire for the inner cleansing and filling of the Spirit of God.

> God led me on Friday morning, simply as a little child, to trust him for this priceless gift, the fullness of the Holy Spirit. By simple, naked faith I took the gift, but I was not conscious of receiving anything. All through that day there seemed a deeper dryness and dullness in one's soul—no new pulsations, no new sense of the presence of God.... Sunday morning just as dry as ever; and the Sunday morning service came, and during the proclamation of the message, there came silently stealing into my heart a strange new sense of ease and rest and peace. That is how it began; and then it deepened, hour by hour during the day, deepened in the evening, and in the after-meeting it seemed to culminate in one great tidal wave of the glory of God that swelled and submerged and interpenetrated, and broke me down in silent, holy adoration in God's presence.[4]

One who knew him well said later:

> Out of that baptism there emerged the apostolic ministry of the sanctified Charles Inwood, and its rivers flowed to the ends of the earth.[5]

Does your heart cry for this? God is no respecter of persons; the Father's promised gift is for all. Believe it is for you!

Problems Of
A Spirit-Filled Ministry

As we saw in Samuel Chadwick's experience of revival, reconciliation is a normal result of a Spirit-filled ministry. Old enemies are reconciled; church splits are healed; antagonists lay down the sword. That type of spiritual and emotional healing can be expected in most cases when the pastor of a church receives the baptism of the Holy Spirit.

---

[4]Samuel Chadwick, *The Call to Christian Perfection* (Kansas City, Mo.: Beacon Hill Press, 1943), p. 73.
[5]Ibid.

However, there may be times when the Holy Spirit's anointing of the pastor tends to bring out the polarities of a congregation. A Spirit-filled pastor may stir up the Devil in a church like nothing else will. Many years ago, I preached for a Methodist pastor in Kansas who said, "Dennis, a personal Pentecost puts you in hell or heaven." He was speaking out of his own hard experience. A Spirit-filled pastor spells the end of the lukewarm church. The mood of his congregation will turn one way or the other, more like heaven or more like hell, and the individuals in that congregation will shift one way or the other.

I know a young woman who prays, "Lord, make me a crisis person so that the people I meet will have to move one way or the other." That's the dynamic you can expect when you begin ministering in the power of the Holy Spirit.

You may be asking at this point, "Why is power needed?" Because if we say that the convicting work of the Holy Spirit begins before an unbeliever sits down in the pew, it would seem that the preacher could deliver the Word of God in a most mechanical, lifeless sort of way and the Holy Spirit could still carry out the work. In that case, why would the preacher need any supernatural power?

I don't think I can tell you all the whys. David Brainerd preached through a drunken interpreter and had Indians converted, so I know it is possible for God to convict the lost through an unconsecrated preacher. Truth is still truth, no matter how dry the form in which it comes; God still can use it for his purpose.

But I believe there is something winsome about the personal impact of a preacher who is in tune with his message, which increases the effectiveness of it. An inkling of this may be found in representational theology, which affirms that the Christian (and in this case, the Christian minister) is representing Christ to the world by his very demeanor as well as by what he says. When the world sees Christ authentically represented, something within the worldly heart says, "Ah ha! I recognize that." Not only must the Word be spoken and the conviction be felt, but the Spirit of Christ must be presented in human form if the gospel is to have its fullest impact upon the unbeliever.

Another fact to consider is that when God is successful in one heart he has greater access to another. There is a cumulative effect when people obey God. Obedience in my life gives God greater leverage on those within my sphere of influence. We may not fully understand the mystery of this, but we should recognize that it is true.

On that first Easter evening, Jesus. said more to his disciples about their need for the Spirit than about the specifics of their witness. He thus implied that their obedience to the Spirit would be their most effective way of winning others to Christ. The history of the church verifies this: The Spirit-filled, Spirit-anointed minister is the most fruitful minister.

Are you filled with the Spirit?

7

Epilogue:
Being With Jesus

We cannot imagine how the disciples of Jesus felt the Saturday and Sunday after the crucifixion. Perhaps no other band of people has ever suffered greater emotional trauma than they! Dismay, despair, and sorrow mingled with their guilt.

The disciples had believed so deeply that Jesus was the One for whom Israel waited. They had believed deeply enough that they left work and family and friends to follow him for three and a half years. They had staked their lives on their belief. And they had loved him.

But now Jesus was gone. He was dead and buried. And with his death went all their hopes. Worse, their trauma was heightened by a sense of guilt. Not one of them had acquitted himself well in those last hours of Jesus' life. Their shame made personal loss and despair even more bitter.

Now some strange stories were circulating among them—stories that Jesus had been seen on that Sunday by some of his friends. As the shadows lengthened into night, those who knew him best sought out one another; when they had found each other, they locked the doors. (Fear was also a part of their suffering.) Quickly, they began to share the experiences of that day. Cleophas and his nameless friend came in from Emmaus; while they were telling their experience of meeting the resurrected Jesus, the miracle occurred.

It really should not have come as a surprise. He had tried to prepare them for it. He had assured them that whenever two or more of them met to talk about him, before they finished he would be there. Suddenly, that promise which always fills true Christian worship with mystery and excitement was fulfilled. He was there, the living Lord in their midst. If the preceding two days had been filled with negative emotions, we can be sure these moments exploded with ecstatic joy. Death had not really contained him. He was alive!

Or was it just an illusion? If it really was Jesus, how should they respond? Loving joy made them want to grasp him and never let him go. But that joy may have been attenuated by guilt. At least Peter may have preferred for the moment to flee.

Yet the disciples were not left in a quandary as to how they should respond. Jesus spoke, and his greeting must have brought them joy: "Peace be with you!" (John 20:19).

John gives a very brief account of the conversation that night. He recalls only five sentences of what Jesus said. Two of those sentences are, "Peace be with you." John also records the fact that when Jesus appeared to them again the next week, he blessed them with the same greeting (v. 26).

Luke was not in that meeting on Easter evening. We do not know who informed him of it; but the informant was also impressed by Jesus' greeting, because Luke also tells us that Jesus stood in their midst and said, "Peace be with you" (Luke 24:36).

These words must have been sweet to the ears of the disciples. Perhaps they heard in them an indication of his will toward them. He did not come to upbraid them because they had failed to believe, nor to chastise them because they had forsaken him. He came to let them know that he was alive and ready to resume the relationship of trust and love that they had known before. His will toward them was good. Little wonder they savored these words and recorded them for us!

Then Jesus showed them his hands and his side. For six months he had been telling them he would suffer and be crucified. Now he showed them the evidence in his resurrected body. When he had spoken to them about the cross, they had been unable to hear him. The cross was unthinkable for them. But Friday had forced home the reality he had foretold. Then the question was, "Why?" Now they looked at his scars and began to come to terms with it all. All that they were later to understand of the atonement undoubtedly had its hesitant beginnings in these moments. Perhaps here for the first time they began to be conscious of the fact that the tragedy of Friday involved them, that it was accomplished for them. Paul later spoke for them all:

> For what I received I passed on to you as of first importance:
> that Christ died for our sins according to the Scriptures...
> (1 Cor. 15:3).

It was not an accident of history nor a fateful tragedy that took Jesus to the Cross. He had done it for them. He had died for their sin. His crucifixion was the supreme evidence of the Father's love.

In that secret room began the church's love affair with the scars of Jesus. If you have any question about this, sing your way through the hymnal and notice how these evidences of God's love have caught the imagination of our hymn writers. All hymns about the crucifixion express our involvement in it. At other events of history, we may stand as spectators; but there we were existentially involved. In fact, we were the chief participants because it was for us that he suffered and died. The scars are eternal witnesses to his love for us:

> Crown Him the Lord of love:
> Behold His hands and side,
> Rich wounds, yet visible above,
> In beauty glorified;
> No angel in the sky
> Can fully bear that sight,
> But downward bends his wondering eye
> At mysteries so bright.

If we think it awesome that the eternal Christ bears forever in his body the marks of his commitment to creatures like us, we can scarcely imagine the mystery of such love to the angels. Note Wesley's famous lines:

> Five bleeding wounds He bears,
>   Received on Calvary;
> They pour effectual prayers,
> They strongly plead for me;
> Forgive him, O forgive, they cry,
> Nor let that ransomed sinner die!

The power of this theme is reflected in a story from the British Methodist, J. E. Rattenbury. In his book, *The Eucharistic Hymns of John and Charles Wesley*, Rattenbury tells of the impact this hymn had upon him when he was a child. Hymns written specifically for children never seemed to grip him; but this one did. The first verse particularly caught his attention:

> Arise, my soul, arise,
> Shake off thy guilty fears;
> The bleeding Sacrifice
> In my' behalf appears:
> Before the Throne my Surety stands;
> My name is written on His hands.

With the tender conscience of a child, Rattenbury knew what "guilty fears" were. So he felt this hymn applied to his own life. But the last line particularly fired his imagination: "My name is written on His hands." The only writing on human flesh that Rattenbury had ever seen was tattooing on the body of a sailor; so he wondered if his name was tattooed on the hands of Jesus, an indication of Christ's love for him and commitment to him, in spite of his guilt.

It is a moving thought. There are some days when I know I have not acted as I ought, when I have been more like the forlorn disciples on Easter night than I would like to admit. I can almost hear the heavenly Father ask Jesus, "'Son, how did that Kinlaw guy do today?" I hear the Son respond, "Well, Father, he did not do so well today...."

I quake as I hear the Father say, "Shall we give up on him?" But then my spirit leaps with Rattenbury's when, in my imagination, I see Jesus lift two scarred hands to the Father and say, "No, Father. We have a substantial investment in him. We are not going to give up on him."

I find that I too have a love affair with those scars!

God in his wisdom has seen to it that the church will have difficulty forgetting the message of the scars. He has built into the life and liturgy of the church a bit of the drama that makes this message inescapable. Every time a pastor says, "This is my body which was broken for you.... And this is my blood which was shed for you," we are reminded that Christ's will toward us is good.

A lady whom I did not know appeared in a Bible class I was teaching and began challenging me quite vigorously at several points. It quickly became evident that, although she had a religious background, she understood little of the historic orthodox Christian faith. For example, in one class session she said, "Dennis, this 'love of Jesus' bit nauseates me. When you speak of the 'love for God,' I can live with that. But the 'love of Jesus' repels me."

She kept coming to class, though. One Sunday at lunch time she phoned to ask if I could come to her house immediately. When I entered her home, she met me with eyes full of tears. I was not quite prepared for what she said: "I see it, Dennis. For the first time, I see it." She was obviously quite moved.

"What do you see, Sylvia?" I responded.

"I see that he did it for me! I never saw it until this morning. He did it for me!"

Communion had been served in her church that morning. She had sat in the choir and listened to the familiar words of Scripture while her pastor broke the bread and lifted the cup. And suddenly, for the first time in her life, she saw the truth. The "love of Jesus" was no longer a nauseating sentiment; it was an historical reality, represented now in the body of her risen Lord. The love symbolized there, now seen, evoked her love and adoration.

Yes, the moments Jesus spent with his disciples that first Easter evening must have been very tender and precious.

"I Am Sending You"

Then Jesus spoke again. Perhaps no words in all of Scripture are more shocking than the ones that now fell on the disciples' ears. While the scars spoke of Christ's will *toward* them, he now spoke of his will *for* them: "As the Father has sent me, I am sending you" (John 20:21).

We should not be too critical of the disciples for failing to grasp immediately the import of these words. The evidence shows that the church still has not heard all that Jesus was saying here. Yet this is his most moving statement of our mission.

This commission is keenly appropriate for the Gospel of John, for a careful reading shows that the concept of "sentness" is central to this Gospel. The two Greek words for "sent" (ἀποστέλλω and πέμπω) are used about forty times in John; both are found in this verse. Jesus' use of these words reveals the profound awareness of mission that he had, the acute sense of "sentness." They are expressive of how Jesus saw his relationship to the Father and to the world. His expression in Greek literally means, "the sending-me Father" (8:16, 18 et al). This sense of mission had been determinative of Jesus' entire life. Now he turned to that band of disciples huddled together in a secret room on Easter evening and said, "As the Father has sent me, I am sending you."

In this way, Jesus spells out the Christians' commission in the world. We are to be to the world something of what Jesus is to us. He came to redeem the world; having finished the earthly part of that commission, he sends us as his co-workers to complete the job. Yes, he calls us to work *with* him as well as for him.

What a job! If every person is as big as his job, then Christians should stand tall. We are engaged in the most vital business in the world, God's business. This is why there is always something regal about the person who obeys God's call and gives herself or himself to the task of reaching the world.

However, we should carefully note to whom Jesus speaks here. Not only were the apostles in that room. Cleophas and his nameless friend were there; the women who had found Jesus' tomb that morning also were there. To all of them, he gave the same commission that he had received from his Father. Jesus was sent so that the world would not perish, but be saved. Now he sent his own with the same commission.

This has profound vocational implications for all who claim the name of Christ. Every person has the right to choose whether to become a Christian. Once a person has chosen, though, he finds that he has made another decision. His business is now to finish the ministry which Christ began. What a responsibility!

Of course, this does not obscure the fact that there are orders of ministry. Some are called to be pastors, others to be teachers, others to be evangelists, still others to be missionaries, and so on. Some are called to be bankers, some to be lawyers, some to be farmers, some to be wives and mothers. But a Christian's place of ministry—a Christian's role—is not the determinative factor of his life. His *call* is what counts, and it is universally the same for every Christian. God calls every Christian with Christ to the task of saving the world. What a task!

But what a relationship accompanies the task! A close study of John's Gospel is most revealing in this regard. Notice:

• Christ sends the Church as the Father sends him.

• Christ's "sentness" reflects his relationship to the Father. Our "sentness" indicates a similar relationship to Christ.

• Now the relationship that Christ has with us, we have with the world.

What Jesus means to the church, the church is supposed to mean to the world. What a relationship indeed!

And what an intimacy! A study of the Gospels will reveal a close intimacy of the Father and the Son, which is witnessed by many texts. At the baptism of Jesus, the Father says:

> You are my Son, whom I love; with you I am well pleased (Mark 1: 11b).

Note that this statement occurs at the precise moment Jesus identifies himself with a sinful world by submitting to baptism. On the Mount of Transfiguration the divine voice speaks again:

> This is my Son, whom I love. Listen to him! (Mark 9:7b).

This statement comes immediately after Jesus' conversation with Elijah and Moses concerning the cross (Luke 9:31). A third time the Gospels report that God's voice was heard authenticating the Father's pleasure with his Son; it is found in John 12:27-28, at the moment Jesus commits himself to go to the cross so that the world might see and know him:

> 'Now my heart is troubled, and what shall I say? "Father, save me from this hour"? No, it was for this very reason I came to this hour. Father, glorify your name' Then a voice came from heaven, 'I have glorified it, and will glorify it again.'

One cannot read the Gospels without sensing the close intimacy that Jesus had with his Father and, conversely, that this intimacy was associated with Jesus' voluntary commitment to the mission on which his Father had sent him. That intimacy is a picture of the intimacy Christ wants with us.

Intimacy And "Sentness"

One evening I spent about four hours with a young missionary who was giving his life for a tribe of primitive Indians in Latin America. He was hardly more than thirty years of age, yet he had been working outside the United States for more than a decade.

In fact, this young man left the university after his sophomore year, liquidated what he owned, and bought a one-way ticket to the mission field. Despite the opposition of his family and without anyone to lend him financial support, he had dropped out of school and gone to foreign mission work. His story was so dramatic that I found it difficult to question the propriety of what he had done. Yet I found myself asking, "Why did you have to go then? Why could you not wait until you had finished your training and secured some support?"

He looked away for a moment. Then he turned as if he had a secret that he was not sure he could entrust to me. He said, "I had found an intimacy with Jesus that I was afraid I would lose if I did not do what he wanted me to do."

You may question his judgment and his timing. But no one who knows the Scriptures can question his insight concerning intimacy with Christ.

In Matthew's account of the Great Commission (28:18-20), Jesus tells his disciples that when they go to disciple the nations he will be with them. As the Father was with Jesus in his "sentness," Jesus promises to be with us in ours. The reason: Jesus has no other way to be in the world except through us. So he has pledged himself to be with us.

But there is a price to be paid for this intimacy. The Bible speaks about our *method* as well as our mission. The world will have to be reached in the same way that we have been reached, through self-giving love. Jesus described it as laying down one's life for his friends:

> I am the good shepherd. The good shepherd lays down his life for the sheep (John 10:11).

Jesus insisted that he was not required to surrender his life:

> No one takes it from me, but I lay it down of my own accord. I have authority to lay it down and authority to take it up again... (John 10:18).

Then he speaks to his disciples:

> My command is this: Love each other as I have loved you.
> Greater love has no one than this, that he lay down his life for
> his friends (John 15:12-13).

In John 17:18 he speaks to his Father about them:

> As you sent me into the world, I have sent them into the
> world.

His method of reaching the world through us is the same as
that used by the Father to reach us through Christ: self-sacrificing
love. This does not mean that our actions have redemptive value in
themselves; it means that Christ's redemptive power becomes effective for others when we give up our rights to ourselves and become
sacrificial instruments of his Spirit. This is costly, but there is no
other way. And saving the world is worth any price, ultimately.

Helen Roseveare spent several years in medical missionary work
in Africa, giving herself for others, until one day she fell into the
hands of rebel soldiers. She was mercilessly beaten and kicked. Her
teeth were broken, her mouth and nose gashed, and her ribs
bruised. When the rebel lieutenant pulled out his gun and pressed
it to her forehead, Helen prayed he would pull the trigger; she
knew that if he did not, worse pain and humiliation lay ahead.

She felt utterly alone. Had God forsaken her? In the loneliness
and humiliation of that moment, his love enveloped her and an
incredible peace flowed through her. Then he spoke:

> These are not your sufferings; they are not beating you. These
> are my sufferings: All I ask of you is the loan of your body.

Then the Lord breathed into Helen's troubled mind the word,
privilege. Note her comment:

> For twenty years, anything I had needed, I had asked of God
> and he had provided. Now, this night, the Almighty had
> stopped to ask of *me* something that he condescended to
> appear to need, and he offered me the *privilege* of responding.
> He wanted my body in which to live, and through which to

love these very rebel soldiers in the height of their wicked-
ness.... He offered me the inestimable privilege of sharing
with him in some little measure, at least, in the edge of the fellowship of his sufferings. And it was all privilege.[1]

Cost swallowed up in privilege! He does that when he sends us
in his place.

Power To Stand
In Christ's Stead

But how can the likes of you and me ever stand in Christ's stead
and do his work? Jesus knew there was only one way, so he spoke
again: "Receive the Holy Spirit" (John 20:22).

The reason for his saying this should be obvious to anyone familiar with the life of Jesus. Jesus did his work through the power of the
Holy Spirit. His ministry began with his baptism at the hands of
John, and on that occasion the Holy Spirit descended upon him
(Mark 1:10; John 1:32-34). Only then was Jesus ready to face the
Tempter and ready to begin his ministry. When the Pharisees ques-
tioned the source of the power that worked within him, Jesus
assured them it was the Holy Spirit (Matt. 12:24-28). How appropriate that on the night before his death Jesus should speak most
fully of that Spirit (John 14-16)! And how appropriate that he
should urge his own disciples not to leave Jerusalem until they had
received the Spirit with his power to live and serve in Christ's stead.
If they were to do his work, they must have his secret; and that
secret to life and service is his Spirit. The Holy Spirit is Christ's *provision* for his servants.

As we noted earlier, it is no accident that the biographies of
those who have been most effective for Christ in their life and service reveal a battle at this point. Just as the unbeliever keeps hoping
he can do something of saving significance by himself, so the believer tends to think that in his own power he can live for Christ and

---

[1]Helen Roseveare, *Living Sacrifice* (Chicago: Moody Press, 1979), pp. 20-21.

serve Christ. But the sanctification of Christ's messenger is a work of grace, mediated by the Spirit, just as much as the justification of the sinner is. So the believer finds that the flesh is as sterile (i.e., unfruitful) after conversion as it was before. Sometime in the believer's life there must be a crucifixion of the self, which brings him to the end of any confidence in himself, if he is to serve God acceptably.

We must come to the end of ourselves so that the Spirit may work without hindrance in our lives.

Consider the witness of Harold Ockenga, one of the most effective contemporary preachers of the gospel. He had been a Christian for some time and was a ministerial student already active in ministry when he became conscious of profound inadequacies in his power to live for Christ and serve him. Ockenga found in his own spirit much that hindered Christ's Spirit. The answer lay in an experience remarkably like Gethsemane and Calvary.

> Something in [him] died that night. It was not reduced; it was crucified. It was not hidden; it was brought forth to be slain. The self life was dealt with just as his sins had been dealt with in salvation. The course of his life changed and from that time onward his one thought was to have the will of God for his life preeminent in every decision. He now could say in simple sincerity, "Not my will but Thy will be done."[2]

Self-will and self-interest are the great enemies of the Spirit in the life of a believer. Cleansing from these by the Spirit frees us to be acceptable instruments of his grace. Oh, that all of us who bear his Word would not only let the Spirit give new life through new birth but also cleanse our spirits until we are emptied of self-interest, so that he *reigns* within! Effective Christian living and serving begins with Christ's provision for us: his Spirit.

---

[2]Harold Lindsell, *Park Street Prophet* (Wheaton, Ill.: Van Kampen Press, 1951), p. 30.

The Minister
An Instrument Of Forgiveness

Christ now speaks a final word, which concerns forgiveness. The language may be a bit difficult for some; but its meaning within the context of the gospel is clear. Christ came to bring forgiveness of sins. If we are to be sent in his place, then we too become instruments through which God's forgiveness comes to the world:

> If you forgive anyone his sins, they are forgiven; if you do not forgive them, they are not forgiven (John 20:23).

We cannot forgive sins. Only God can do that. But we can be the means through which the gospel of forgiveness comes to a sinful world. We must remember that we are here in Christ's stead.

I believe the verse might be paraphrased like this: "I am giving the gospel to you. If you will give it to others, they will be able to experience the forgiveness of sin. But if you do not give it to others, they will perish. As you share the gospel, therefore, the gates of heaven will be opened to those with whom you share it. But as you refuse to share it, the gates of heaven will be closed because you refused to give the world an opportunity to respond to the truth."

If Christ had not obeyed his Father, you and I would not be redeemed from our sins. Now you and I stand in Christ's stead; if we do not obey him, the world will not be redeemed. Might that be why so much of the world languishes without Christ—because we have not obeyed him? Sharing the gospel is not the only thing Christ expects us to do; but it is the first thing.

The surprise in this passage is that Christ speaks only of forgiveness. Is evangelism, leading people to find forgiveness of their sins, the sole business of the church? Why did He not speak of more? The church surely has a broader ministry than this. What of services to the poor, the sick, and the oppressed? What of Christian education? Are there not other ministries, too?

Christ's word must be taken in its larger context. After all, the One who speaks here so exclusively about forgiveness has already spent several years in ministry, during which he fed the hungry, healed the sick, and delivered the oppressed. Lest anyone think that Jesus evidences no concern for social problems, let us remember that he is responsible for every good thing which life can give. He speaks here only in terms of priority. He wants his church to do many things; but one thing is primary. That one thing was the prime reason for his passion.

Many benefits come from the cross. But the first benefit, witnessed by the Lord's Supper, is the forgiveness of sins. Evangelism is not the sole business of the church, but it is the first. Certainly, it is the first business of a Spirit-filled preacher.

INDEX